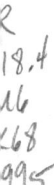

W0017617

Contents

Acknowledgments   v

Introduction   vii

Subject Finder   1

Hotlines   7

National Health and
  Health-Related
  Organizations   11

ALA FINGERTIP GUIDE TO

● ● ● ● ● ● ● ● ● ● ● ● ● ●

National Health-Information Resources

1995–1996
Reference Desk Edition

Beatrice
Kovacs

AMERICAN LIBRARY ASSOCIATION
Chicago and London 1995

Series editor: Sheila S. Intner

Design and composition by Charles Bozett

Printed on 50-pound Thor D-48 Offset, a pH-neutral stock, and bound in 10-point C1S cover stock by Malloy Lithographic, Inc.

The paper used in this publication meets the minimum requirements of American National Standard for Information Sciences—Permanence of Paper for Printed Library Materials, ANSI Z39.48-1992. ∞

Library of Congress Cataloging-in-Publication Data

Kovacs, Beatrice
    ALA fingertip guide to national health-information resources / [compiled] by Beatrice Kovacs. — 1995–1996 reference desk ed.
        p. cm.
    Includes index.
    ISBN 0-8389-0645-1 (acid-free paper)
    1. Medicine—United States—Information services—Directories. 2. Medical care—United States—Information services—Directories. 3. Diseases—United States—Information services—Directories. 4. Health—Information services—Directories. I. Title.
R118.4.U6K68   1994
025.06′ 61′02573—dc20   94-38095

Printed in the United States of America

99 98 97 96 95   5 4 3 2 1

Acknowledgments

Without the assistance of several people, this directory could not have been completed for timely publication. I would like to take this opportunity to thank my graduate assistants, Stephen Strother and John Barnett, for their diligence and patience in verifying or re-verifying many addresses and telephone numbers. I truly appreciate the work they have done on this project. Also, without the assistance and support of the faculty in the Department of Library and Information Studies, School of Education, University of North Carolina at Greensboro, and especially Marilyn Miller, for providing the resources needed, I could not have completed this book.

The publication of this work is the result of encouragement I received from Sheila S. Intner, to expand a resource list I had compiled into a handy directory. Art Plotnik, of ALA Editions, helped make it possible. I thank both of them for their belief in this work. The suggestions from P. Gayle Alston were deeply appreciated, also.

I must also thank my husband, Louis E. Mitchum, for his support during the creation of this directory. His willingness to assume everyday duties enabled me to concentrate on finishing quickly.

Finally, thank you to Helen Kovacs, my mother and retired medical librarian, who taught me the importance of information to society. She believed in this project and insisted that I complete it. I miss you, Mom.

Introduction

The purpose of this directory is to gather, in one handy location, up-to-date names, addresses, and telephone numbers of a variety of health-related service organizations. It was prompted by the ever-increasing interest in personal and societal health, fueled by the debate over health and health care provision in the United States.

If we want to know more about conditions that affect our lives, or treatment possibilities and alternatives, or any other aspect of health-related information, we can contact many specialists and experts for free advice. A number of excellent tools already exist to identify appropriate telephone numbers, including commonly available sources such as local telephone directories. Usually, however, these list only an agency's local chapter, which cannot always meet our information needs. We need to know national or international headquarters' telephone numbers and addresses.

The difficulty in creating a printed national directory is keeping it up-to-date. The mobility of our society makes this a challenging task. All of the addresses and telephone numbers listed in this directory were verified between April and August 1994. However, of the 250 identified and verified in August of 1993, by April 1994 16 (or 6.4%) had moved. When upcoming relocation was mentioned, the new address was included in this work. It is likely, however, that many addresses and telephone numbers will change again in the near future. Therefore, we expect to update this directory within two years, if interest warrants. Special emphasis has been placed on those organizations with toll-free telephone numbers, although many have been included which do not offer such service because they are of interest to the general public. Additionally, only those organizations which are nationwide have been included. There are many fine organizations that have regional or statewide service areas, but these have been omitted in this directory because the scope is national.

No attempt has been made to critically evaluate the organization or agency, nor has there been judgment beyond public interest regarding the subject scope for inclusion or exclusion. Traditional and alternative health practices are included, because the interest of the public follows all paths. The American Library Association, in publishing the work, furthers its interest in the broadest public access to sources of information. Please note, however, that inclusion in this directory is not an endorsement of the agency or its work. Conversely, criticism should not be assumed against agencies excluded from this directory. There may have been problems, instead, in verifying addresses or telephone numbers, or some other reason an organization was not included.

We would appreciate any suggestions for additional organizations or agencies to be included in this directory, as well as requests for helpful types of information. Your comments would also be helpful about our plans to include Internet addresses, fax numbers, and services provided for the non–English-speaking public. Recommendations should be sent to Beatrice Kovacs, associate professor, Department of Library and Information Studies, School of Education, University of North Carolina at Greensboro, Greensboro, NC 27412-5001, USA.

Subject Finder

Note: All numbers in this subject index refer to organization numbers in this directory, and *not* to page numbers.

abortion 225

abuse, child *see* child abuse prevention

abuse, familial 152, 395

accident prevention 280, 315

adoption 1, 130, 189, 226, 227

aerobics 4, 137

aging 210, 234, 251, 257

AIDS 10, 72, 111, 114, 128, 228, 241, 277, 285, 298, 300, 317, 340, 353, 378, 393

air ambulance 5, 11, 12, 218

albinism 302

alcoholism 13, 14, 40, 233, 254, 258

alcoholism in the elderly 14

alcoholism in teens 13

allergy 19, 36, 97, 230, 277

alternative medicine or therapeutics 87, 126, 149, 155, 166, 192, 325, 342

Alzheimer's disease 17, 47, 162, 232

ambulances *see* air ambulance

amyotrophic lateral sclerosis 81, 207

anemia 136, 153

anesthesiologists 64

ankylosing spondylitis 82

anorexia nervosa 83, 84, 184

arthritis 87, 88

asbestos 89, 90

asthma 97, 230, 277

atherosclerosis 187

attention-deficit disorder 243

autism 86, 244

automobile safety 280

backache 379

Batten's disease 98

bioenergetic analysis 192

bioethics 309

birth defects 138, 146, 215

blacks (health) 245, 298, 328

blacks in the health professions 248

blindness 41, 45, 91, 102, 103, 110, 211, 240, 251, 267, 320, 354, 359, 361, 402

bone marrow donors 295

Boys Town 154

brain disorders and injuries 246

brain tumors 32

breast cancer 376, 403

breast feeding (La Leche) 206

bulemia 83, 84, 184

bundle branch block 188

burns 345, 365

cancer 18, 33, 46, 51, 106, 107, 108, 123, 247, 269, 277, 346, 376

cardiology 37, 188

CARE 109

cerebral palsy 384

chemicals 115

child abuse prevention 116, 120, 203, 205, 249, 256, 259, 311, 404

childbirth 76, 169, 185, 349

child safety 253

children 30, 93, 94, 102, 108, 116, 117, 118, 119, 120, 121, 122, 147, 154, 155, 169, 172, 175, 189, 236, 282, 283, 339, 340, 365, 373, 383, 386, 404

children, missing 117, 204, 219, 220, 249, 394

chiropractics 34, 337

cleft palate 35, 124

cocaine 125, 255

colitis 141

colorectal diseases 151

conservation of energy 131

consumer education 132, 133, 134, 319

contact lenses 135, 193

Cooley's anemia 136

Cornelia de Lange syndrome 138

coronary see heart and heart diseases

cosmetic surgery 20

counselors 60, 233

craniofacial 35, 119, 235

Crohn's disease 141

cryonics 15

cystic fibrosis 142

DARE 145

deafness 48, 143, 170, 383

death and dying 122, 129, 176

dentistry 2, 42, 149, 183

depressive illness 270

dermatology 21, 197

developmental disorders 144

diabetes mellitus 26, 43, 202

dietetics 44, 377

diets and dieting see weight control

disabled 172, 181, 200, 252, 282, 283, 303, 339, 365

disease control 114
dogs for the blind 165
dogs for the deaf 171
Down syndrome 261, 262
drug abuse 145, 201, 224, 233, 254, 255, 277, 336
drugs, experimental 353
drunk drivers 221
dwarfism 212
dyslexia 331

ear disorders 217
Easter Seal Society 146, 263
eating disorders 83, 84, 184, 332
ecology 163, 370
emergency medicine 264
emotional disorders 144
endometriosis 148
endoscopy 73
environmental health and protection 96, 149, 163, 180, 229, 274, 290, 307, 313, 327, 329, 360, 362, 375, 380
epilepsy 105, 150
ethics, medical 309
experimental drugs *see* drugs, experimental
eye and eye diseases 191, 265, 266

facial surgery 22, 235, 271
family health 139, 152, 154, 259, 395
family physicians 23
Fanconi's anemia 153
fire prevention 268

fitness and fitness professionals 4, 179
Food and Drug Administration 158
food inspection 159
foster home care 118
foundations 160
Fragile X 272

gastrointestinal diseases 73, 141
Gaucher's disease 273
gays 352
genetic diseases 16, 272, 273
glaucoma 47
growth 177
guide dogs *see* dogs for the blind; dogs for the deaf

handicapped 172, 174
handicapped, employment 200, 267
hazardous waste 6, 7, 8, 9, 104, 313, 391
head injury 275
headache 276
health 3, 6, 8, 95, 134, 161, 163, 166, 277, 334, 341, 342, 400, 401
health assistance 47, 109, 319
health education 7
health insurance 168, 296
hearing 48, 78, 100, 170, 237, 278, 326, 383
heart and heart diseases 47, 49
hematology 198

hemophilia 279
hepatitis 56
herbalism 157
herpes 72
histiocytosis 175
holistic health 50
homeless 140, 312
hospice 121, 176, 281, 286
hospitality houses 238
Huntington's chorea 178
hydrocephalus 164
hypopigmentation 302

immunology 19, 36, 288
impotence 356
incontinence 173, 367
insurance 52, 168, 347
internal medicine 74

kidney and kidney disease
    27, 54, 289

Lamaze (ASPO) 76
lead 290
legal medicine 38
leprosy 55
lesbians 352
leukemia 208, 209, 292
leukodystrophy 385
liver 56
Lou Gehrig's disease see
    amyotrophic lateral
    sclerosis
lung 57
lupus 58, 214
lymphedema 293

managed care 53, 239
Marfan syndrome 294

marrow donors 295
maternity homes 147
Medicare 74, 277, 390
medicine 59, 346
medicine, alternative see
    alternative medicine
medicine, internal see
    internal medicine
medicine, legal see legal
    medicine
medicine, osteopathic see
    osteopathic medicine
medicine, preventive see
    preventive medicine
medicine, respiratory see
    respiratory medicine
mental health and illness
    60, 127, 144, 190, 231,
    232, 297, 312, 355, 400
mental retardation 28, 272
minority health 245, 298,
    328
multiple sclerosis 299
muscular dystrophy 222
myasthenia gravis 223

Native Americans 300
neurofibromatosis 301
nurses and nursing 61, 291
nurses, visiting 397
nutrition 182, 346

obstetrics 76
occupational health and
    safety 96, 113, 287
ophthalmology 333
optometry 62
organ donation 213, 216,
    295, 387

orthodontics 29
orthokeratology 193
orthopedics 365
osteopathic medicine 63, 64
osteoporosis 305

pain 186
paralysis 65
parenting 99, 130, 169, 335, 349, 381
Parkinson's disease 66, 306, 338
patient education 134, 260
pediatrics 24
personality assessment 112
pesticides 307, 343
pharmaceutics 67, 350, 392
pharmacy 344, 350
physicians 39, 92, 239, 346, 347
plastic surgeons and surgery 22, 75
podiatry 25, 330
polio 194, 351
polyposis 151
pregnancy 99, 156
preventive medicine 52, 182, 346
Project HOPE 341
psychiatry 30, 68
psychology 69, 112
psychoprophylaxis in obstetrics 76

radon 308, 390
rare diseases 304
reconstructive surgeons and surgery 22, 75

Red Cross 70
rehabilitation 71, 195, 310, 357
relief programs 70, 109, 386
research, medical 358
respiratory medicine 199, 288
retardation 85, 91, 94
retinitis pigmentosa 361
retirement 31
Reye's syndrome 314
Rhett's syndrome 196
runaways 219

safety 315, 389
safety, automobile *see* automobile safety
safety, food *see* food inspection
safety, occupational *see* occupational health and safety
sarcoidosis 316
scleroderma 363, 364, 388
sclerosis, amyotropic lateral *see* amyotrophic lateral sclerosis
sclerosis, multiple *see* multiple sclerosis
sclerosis, tuberous *see* tuberous sclerosis
sexually transmitted diseases 72
shelters 140
sickle cell disease 242
Sjogren's syndrome 318
smoking cessation 368
social health 72

social security 369
spasmodic torticollis 321
speech 237
spina bifida 371
spinal cord injuries 65, 322, 372
spondylitis, ankylosing *see* ankylosing spondylitis
sports medicine 399
stroke 49, 323
Sturge-Weber syndrome 374
stuttering 250
substance abuse 152
sudden infant death syndrome 77, 366
surgery 20, 21, 22, 92, 197, 271

tinnitus 78
Tourette syndrome 382
toxicology 9, 274
transplantation 348
trauma 79
tuberous sclerosis 324

tumors, brain *see* brain tumors

UNICEF 386
urologic diseases 46

venereal diseases 72, 111
veterans, blind 103
veterans, Vietnam 284
veterinary medicine 50, 80
vision 101, 102, 251, 396
visiting nurses 397
volunteerism, health 167
von Recklinghausen's disease *see* neurofibromatosis

waste 6, 7, 8, 9, 104, 329, 375, 391
water 6, 274, 362
weight control 377
wellness 325, 398
women 399
women, black 245
workman's compensation 53

Hotlines

(alphabetically by name)

The following hotlines or information lines for the public have specific names by which they are identified. **Note:** Index numbers refer to the organization numbers in this directory, *not* to page numbers.

9-LINE CRISIS COUNSEL-
ING HOTLINE 140

ABORTION HOTLINE
225

AIDS CLINICAL TRIALS
INFORMATION 285

AIR AMBULANCE TRANS-
PORT 5

AL-ANON, ALATEEN FAMILY
GROUP HOTLINE 13

ALCOHOLISM HOPELINE
258

ALLERGY AND ASTHMA
NETWORK 230

ALLERGY INFORMATION
REFERRAL LINE 19

ANAD HOTLINE (Anorexia
Nervosa and Associated Disorders) 84

ASBESTOS OMBUDSMAN
HOTLINE 89

ASPO LAMAZE 76

AUTO SAFETY HOTLINE
280

BACK PAIN HOTLINE 379

BIOETHICS REFERENCE
CENTER 309

BOYS TOWN NATIONAL
HOTLINE 154

CANCER INFORMATION
AND COUNSELING 18

CANCER INFORMATION
SERVICE 106, 247

CHEMICAL INFORMATION
HOTLINE 115

CLEFTLINE 35

COMMUNITY RIGHT-TO-
KNOW HOTLINES 104,
391

CONSERVATION AND
RENEWABLE ENERGY
HOTLINE 131

CONSUMER HELPLINE (AAO) 29

CONSUMER HELPLINE (NAHSA) 237

CONSUMER PRODUCT SAFETY HOTLINE 389

COSMETIC SURGERY ADVICE 20

DARE AMERICA 145

DIAL-A-HEARING SCREENING TEST 326

DRUG DEPENDENT HOPELINE 258

DWARF HELPLINE 212

ECOLINE 380

ELDERCARE LOCATOR 234

EMERGENCY PLANNING HOTLINES (EPA) 104, 391

ENDOMETRIOSIS CRISIS COUNSELING 148

EPILEPSY INFORMATION SERVICE 105

EXPERIMENTAL DRUGS HOTLINE 353

FACES RESOURCE FILES 235

FACIAL PLASTIC SURGERY INFORMATION SERVICE 22

FAMILIAL POLYPOSIS REGISTRY 151

FAMILY HELPLINE (NHIF) 275

FITNESS INFORMATION LINE 4

HANDI INFORMATION LINE 279

HEARING AID HELPLINE 278

HEARING HELPLINE 100

HELPLINE (Child Abuse and Family Violence) 259

HEPATITIS HOTLINE 56

HERPES RESOURCE CENTER HOTLINE 72

HIT HOME HOTLINE 404

HIV/AIDS STATISTICS INFORMATION LINE 114

HIV-AIDS TREATMENT INFORMATION SERVICE 393

HIV TELEPHONE CONSULTATION SERVICE 128

HOPELINE (National Council on Alcoholism) 258

HOSPICELINK 176

INDIAN AIDS NETWORK 300

JOB ACCOMMODATION NETWORK 200

JOB OPPORTUNITIES FOR THE BLIND 267

LUNG LINE INFORMATION SERVICE 288

MEAT AND POULTRY FOOD SAFETY HOTLINE 159

MEDIC ALERT ORGAN DONOR PROGRAM 216

MEDICAL AND SURGICAL EYE CARE FOR THE ELDERLY 265

MEDICARE HOTLINE 390

MISSING CHILDREN HOTLINE 117

NATIONAL ABORTION FEDERATION HOTLINE 225

NATIONAL AIDS HOTLINES 72

NATIONAL CHILD ABUSE
HOTLINE 116
NATIONAL CHILDWATCH
CAMPAIGN 253
NATIONAL COCAINE HOT-
LINE 255
NATIONAL RADON HOT-
LINE 308
NATIONAL RUNAWAY
SWITCHBOARD 219
NATIONAL SEXUALLY
TRANSMITTED DISEASES
HOTLINE 72
NATIONAL YOUTH CRISIS
HOTLINE 404
NETWORK FOR DISABLED
SEEKING EMPLOYMENT
200
NUTRITION AND HEALTH
161
NUTRITION HOTLINE
(ADA) 44
NUTRITION HOTLINE
(AICR) 51

ORGAN DONOR HOTLINE
387
ORGAN DONOR REGISTRY
AND REFERRAL SERVICE
213
OUST HOTLINE 329

PATIENT AIRLIFT HOTLINE
218

PHARMACY ASSISTANCE
SERVICES 344
PLASTIC SURGERY INFOR-
MATION LINE 75
POSITIVE PREGNANCY AND
PARENTING FITNESS 99
PREGNANCY HOTLINE 156

RCRA (Research Conservation
and Recovery Act) HOT-
LINE 360
REYE'S SYNDROME INFOR-
MATION HOTLINE 314

SAFE DRINKING WATER
HOTLINE 362
SOS RADON 308
SPINAL CORD INJURY HOT-
LINES 65
STROKE CONNECTION 49
SUPERFUND HOTLINE 375

TEL-ROMP 356

U.S. LIVES INFORMATION
LINE 346
US TOO LINE 46

VICTIM HOTLINE (MADD)
221

Y-ME HOTLINE 403

National Health and Health-Related Organizations

1
ADOPTION

AASK America
2201 Broadway, Suite 702
Oakland, CA 94612
(800) 232-2751
   Adopt-A-Special-Kid provides information on adoption of children with special needs.

2
DENTISTRY

Academy of Dentistry International
5125 MacArthur Boulevard NW, No. 50
Washington, DC 20016
(202) 364-8349

3
HEALTH

Advantage Healthcare Net
401 Demers Avenue, Suite 314
Grand Forks, ND 50201
(800) 548-2744
(701) 772-0471

4
AEROBICS;
FITNESS AND
FITNESS
PROFESSIONALS

Aerobics and Fitness Foundation of
         America
15250 Ventura Boulevard, Suite 200
Sherman Oaks, CA 91403
(800) 233-4886 FITNESS INFORMATION LINE
(818) 905-0040

5
AIR AMBULANCE

Aeronational
P.O. Box 538
Washington, PA 15301
(800) 245-9987 AIR AMBULANCE TRANSPORT

6
HAZARDOUS WASTE; HEALTH; WASTE; WATER

Agency for Toxic Substances and Disease
      Registry
Division of Health Assessment and
      Consultation
Executive Park, Building 31, Room 3134
1600 Clifton Road (E33)
Atlanta, GA 30333
(404) 639-0610

7
HAZARDOUS WASTE; HEALTH EDUCATION; WASTE

Agency for Toxic Substances and Disease
      Registry
Division of Health Education
Executive Park, Building 4, Room 1104
1600 Clifton Road (E33)
Atlanta, GA 30333
(404) 639-6204

8
HAZARDOUS WASTE; HEALTH; WASTE

Agency for Toxic Substances and Disease
      Registry
Division of Health Studies
Executive Park, Building 4, Room 1117
1600 Clifton Road (E33)
Atlanta, GA 30333
(404) 639-6200

9
HAZARDOUS WASTE; TOXICOLOGY; WASTE

Agency for Toxic Substances and Disease
      Registry
Division of Toxicology
Executive Park, Building 4, Room 2449
1600 Clifton Road (E33)
Atlanta, GA 30333
(404) 639-6300

10 AIDS	AIDS Clinical Trials Information Service P.O. Box 6421 Rockville, MD 20849-6421 (800) 874-2572 (800) 243-7012 TTY/TDD (301) 217-0023 INTERNATIONAL CALLS (301) 496-8210
11 AIR AMBULANCE	Air Ambulance America 5804 Sunset Drive Miami, FL 33143 (800) 262-8526
12 AIR AMBULANCE	AirLifeLine 1716 X Street Sacramento, CA 95818 (800) 446-1231 (916) 446-0995
13 ALCOHOLISM; ALCOHOLISM IN TEENS	Al-Anon, Alateen Family Group Hotline P.O. Box 862 Midtown Station New York, NY 10018-0862 (800) 344-2666 MEETING INFORMATION ONLY
14 ALCOHOLISM; ALCOHOLISM IN THE ELDERLY	Alcohol Rehabilitation for the Elderly P.O. Box 267 Hopedale, IL 61747 (800) 354-7089
15 CRYONICS	ALCOR Life Extension Foundation 7895 East Acoma Drive, Suite 110 Scottsdale, AZ 85260-6916 (800) 367-2228 INFORMATION AND OUTREACH (602) 922-9013

Provides information about cryonics, or freezing a deceased person in hopes that at some future time the deceased can be revived and cured.

16
GENETIC
DISEASES

Alliance of Genetic Support Groups
35 Wisconsin Circle, Suite 440
Chevy Chase, MD 20815
(800) 336-4363 PUBLICATIONS LIST,
    INFORMATION
(202) 331-0942

Alsac-St. Jude Children's Research
    Hospital
  see St. Jude Children's Research
    Hospital

17
ALZHEIMER'S
DISEASE

Alzheimer's Association
919 North Michigan Avenue, Suite 1000
Chicago, IL 60611-1676
(800) 272-3900 FOR BROCHURE
(800) 621-0379 INFORMATION
(312) 335-8700

Alzheimer's Disease Research
  see American Health Assistance
    Foundation

Alzheimer's Family Relief Program
  see American Health Assistance
    Foundation

18
CANCER

AMC Cancer Information and
    Counseling Line
1600 Pierce Street
Denver, CO 80214
(800) 525-3777 CANCER INFORMATION
    AND COUNSELING

19
ALLERGY;
IMMUNOLOGY

American Academy of Allergy and
    Immunology
611 East Wells Street
Milwaukee, WI 53202
(800) 822-2762 ALLERGY INFORMATION
    REFERRAL LINE
(414) 272-6071

20
COSMETIC
SURGERY;
SURGERY

American Academy of Cosmetic Surgery
401 North Michigan Avenue
Chicago, IL 60611-4267
(800) 221-9808 COSMETIC SURGERY ADVICE
    (Recording)
(312) 644-6610
  Note: The Cosmetic Surgery Advice
consists of a recording that suggests you
consult your doctor or local surgeon;
there is no operator or other individual
with whom to speak.

21
DERMATOLOGY;
SURGERY

American Academy of Dermatology
930 North Meacham Road
Schaumburg, IL 60173-4965
(800) 441-2737 INFORMATION
(708) 330-9830 AMERICAN SOCIETY FOR
    DERMATOLOGIC SURGERY
(708) 330-0230 AMERICAN ACADEMY OF
    DERMATOLOGY
  The non-800 numbers provide physi-
cian referral and surgery referral lines.

22
FACIAL SURGERY;
PLASTIC SUR-
GEONS AND
SURGERY;
RECONSTRUCTIVE
SURGEONS AND
SURGERY;
SURGERY

American Academy of Facial Plastic and
    Reconstructive Surgery
1110 Vermont Avenue NW, Suite 220
Washington, DC 20005-3522
(800) 332-3223 FACIAL PLASTIC SURGERY
    INFORMATION SERVICE
(800) 532-3223 CANADA
(202) 842-4500

23
FAMILY PHYSICIANS

American Academy of Family Physicians
8880 Ward Parkway
Kansas City, MO 64114-2797
(800) 274-2237
(816) 333-9700

24
PEDIATRICS

American Academy of Pediatrics
141 Northwest Point Boulevard
P.O. Box 927
Elk Grove, IL 60009-0927
(800) 433-9016
(708) 228-5005 PUBLIC INFORMATION AND
EDUCATION

25
PODIATRY

American Association of Colleges of
Podiatric Medicine
1350 Piccard Drive, Suite 322
Rockville, MD 20850
(800) 922-9266
(301) 990-7400

26
DIABETES MELLITUS

American Association of Diabetes
Educators
444 North Michigan Avenue, Suite 1240
Chicago, IL 60611
(800) 338-3633
(312) 644-2233

27
KIDNEY AND KIDNEY DISEASE

American Association of Kidney Patients
100 South Ashley Drive, Suite 280
Tampa, FL 33602
(800) 749-2257
(813) 223-7099

28
MENTAL RETARDATION

American Association on Mental
Retardation
444 North Capitol Street, NW, Suite 846
Washington, DC 20001-1570
(800) 424-3688
(202) 387-1968

29
ORTHODONTICS

American Association of Orthodontists
401 North Lindbergh Boulevard
St. Louis, MO 63141
(800) 222-9969 CONSUMER HELPLINE
    (For orders only)
(800) 424-2841

30
CHILDREN;
PSYCHIATRY

American Association for Psychiatric
    Services for Children
1200-C Scottsville Road, Suite 225
Rochester, NY 14624
(800) 777-6910
(716) 235-6910

31
RETIREMENT

American Association of Retired Persons
601 E Street, NW
Washington, DC 20049
(800) 424-2277
(202) 434-2277

32
BRAIN TUMORS

American Brain Tumor Association
2720 River Road, Suite 146
Des Plaines, IL 60018
(708) 827-9910

33
CANCER

American Cancer Society
1599 Clifton Road, NE
Atlanta, GA 30329
(800) 227-2345
(404) 320-3333

34
CHIROPRACTICS

American Chiropractic Association
1701 Clarendon Boulevard
Arlington, VA 22209-2721
(800) 986-4636 INFORMATION
(800) 368-3083 PUBLICATION ORDERS
(703) 276-8800
    Provides information about a theory
of healing that disease results from a
lack of normal nerve function which

can be cured through physical manipulation and adjustment of the spine.

35
CLEFT PALATE;
CRANIOFACIAL

American Cleft Palate-Craniofacial
    Association
1218 Grandview Avenue
Pittsburgh, PA 15211
(800) 242-5338 CLEFTLINE
(412) 481-1376

36
ALLERGY;
IMMUNOLOGY

American College of Allergy and
    Immunology
85 West Algonquin Road, Suite 550
Arlington Heights, IL 60005
(800) 842-7777
(708) 427-1200

37
CARDIOLOGY

American College of Cardiology
9111 Old Georgetown Road
Bethesda, MD 20814
(800) 253-4636
(301) 897-5400

38
LEGAL MEDICINE

American College of Legal Medicine
611 East Wells Street
Milwaukee, WI 53202
(800) 433-9137
(414) 276-1881
    Supports centers for study and
research about medicine and the law,
arranges meetings between medical or
legal groups and judicial or enforcement
groups. Comprised of individuals with
both medical and law degrees.

39
PHYSICIANS

American College of Physicians
Independence Mall West
6th Street at Race
Philadelphia, PA 19106-1572
(800) 523-1546 MEMBER USE ONLY
(215) 351-2400

This association of physicians who
specialize in internal medicine and
related disciplines sponsors courses,
teaching and research scholarships,
and certifies members.

40
ALCOHOLISM

American Council on Alcoholism
5024 Campbell Boulevard, Suite H-1
Baltimore, MD 21236-6950
(800) 527-5344 INFORMATION AND
                REFERRAL LINE
(410) 931-9393

41
BLINDNESS

American Council of the Blind
1155 15th Street, NW, Suite 720
Washington, DC 20005
(800) 424-8666
(202) 467-5081

42
DENTISTRY

American Dental Association
211 East Chicago Avenue
Chicago, IL 60611
(312) 440-2500

43
DIABETES
MELLITUS

American Diabetes Association
1660 Duke Street
Alexandria, VA 22314
(800) 232-3472
(703) 549-1500

44
DIETETICS

American Dietetic Association
216 West Jackson Boulevard, Suite 800
Chicago, IL 60606-6995
(800) 366-1655 NUTRITION HOTLINE
(312) 899-0040
  Registered dieticians are available for consultation and advice.

45
BLINDNESS

American Foundation for the Blind
15 West 16th Street
New York, NY 10011
(800) 232-5463 INFORMATION LINE
    (Recording)
(800) 829-0500 CONSUMER PRODUCTS
    CATALOG AND ORDER PLACEMENT
(212) 620-2000

46
CANCER;
UROLOGIC
DISEASES

American Foundation for Urologic
    Disease
300 West Pratt Street, Suite 401
Baltimore, MD 21201
(800) 242-2383
(800) 828-7866 US TOO LINE
(301) 727-2908
  The "Us Too" line provides information and referral for family members, victims, and other individuals concerned with prostate cancer.

47
ALZHEIMER'S
DISEASE;
GLAUCOMA;
HEALTH
ASSISTANCE;
HEART AND
HEART DISEASES

American Health Assistance Foundation
15825 Shady Grove Road, Suite 140
Rockville, MD 20850
(800) 437-2423
(301) 948-3244
  Includes Alzheimer's Family Relief Program, Alzheimer's Disease Research, Coronary Heart Disease Research, and National Glaucoma Research.

48
DEAFNESS;
HEARING

American Hearing Research Foundation
55 East Washington Street, Suite 2022
Chicago, IL 60602
(312) 726-9670

49
HEART AND
HEART DISEASES;
STROKE

American Heart Association
7272 Greenville Avenue
Dallas, TX 75231-4596
(800) 242-8721
(800) 553-6321 STROKE CONNECTION
(214) 373-6300

50
HOLISTIC HEALTH;
VETERINARY
MEDICINE

American Holistic Veterinary Medical
    Association
c/o Dr. Carvel Tiekert
2214 Old Emmorton Road
Bel Air, MD 21015
(410) 569-0795

51
CANCER

American Institute for Cancer Research
1759 R Street, NW
Washington, DC 20009
(800) 843-8114 NUTRITION HOTLINE
(202) 328-7744

52
INSURANCE;
PREVENTIVE
MEDICINE

American Institute for Preventive
    Medicine
30445 Northwestern Highway, Suite 350
Farmington Hills, MI 48334
(800) 345-2476
(313) 539-1800

53
MANAGED CARE;
WORKMAN'S
COMPENSATION

American International Health and
    Rehabilitation Services
30 West Gude Drive, 5th Floor
Rockville, MD 20850-1161
(800) 227-5065
(301) 251-8600

   This organization has two primary
areas of concern: claims and provider

issues, and managed care and work-man's comp issues.

54
KIDNEY AND
KIDNEY DISEASE

American Kidney Fund
6110 Executive Boulevard, Suite 1010
Rockville, MD 20852
(800) 638-8299
(301) 881-3052

55
LEPROSY

American Leprosy Missions
1 ALM Way
Greenville, SC 29601
(800) 543-3131
(803) 271-7040

56
HEPATITIS; LIVER

American Liver Foundation
1425 Pompton Avenue
Cedar Grove, NJ 07009
(800) 223-0179 HEPATITIS HOTLINE
(201) 256-2550

57
LUNG

American Lung Association
1740 Broadway
New York, NY 10019-4374
(212) 315-8700

58
LUPUS

American Lupus Society
3914 Del Amo Boulevard, Suite 922
Torrance, CA 90503
(800) 331-1802 INFORMATION LINE
(Recording)
(310) 542-8891

59
MEDICINE

American Medical Association
515 North State Street
Chicago, IL 60610
(312) 464-5000

60
COUNSELORS;
MENTAL HEALTH
AND ILLNESS

American Mental Health Counselors
    Association
5999 Stevenson Avenue
Alexandria, VA 22304
(800) 326-2642
(703) 823-9800

American Mental Health Fund
    see National Mental Health Association

61
NURSES AND
NURSING

American Nurses Association
600 Maryland Avenue, SW
Suite 100 West
Washington, DC 20024
(800) 274-4262 MARKETING DEPARTMENT
(800) 284-2378 CERTIFICATION HOTLINE
(800) 637-0323 PUBLICATIONS FOR
    PURCHASE
(202) 651-7000
   While the American Nurses Association is not equipped to handle consumer requests, the public can purchase some of their publications, and ANA may be able to assist with certification questions.

62
OPTOMETRY

American Optometric Association
243 North Lindbergh Boulevard
St. Louis, MO 63141-7881
(800) 262-2210 PROFESSIONAL ORDERS
    ONLY
(314) 991-4100

63
OSTEOPATHIC
MEDICINE

American Osteopathic Association
142 East Ontario Street
Chicago, IL 60611-2818
(800) 621-1773
(312) 280-5800
   Osteopathic medicine is based on the concept that the human body's

musculoskeletal system is a vital part of health, operating in harmony with all other body systems. Doctors of osteopathy can practice in all areas of medicine and surgery, and can prescribe drugs.

64
ANESTHESIOLO-GISTS;
OSTEOPATHIC MEDICINE

American Osteopathic College of Anesthesiologists
17201 East US Highway 40, Suite 204
Independence, MO 64055-6427
(800) 842-2622
(816) 373-4700

65
PARALYSIS;
SPINAL CORD INJURIES

American Paralysis Association
500 Morris Avenue
Springfield, NJ 07081
(800) 225-0292 INFORMATION ON THE ASSOCIATION ONLY
(800) 526-3456 SPINAL CORD INJURY HOTLINES
(201) 379-2690

66
PARKINSON'S DISEASE

American Parkinson Disease Association
60 Bay Street, Suite 401
Staten Island, NY 10301
(800) 223-2732
(718) 981-8001
   Provides help, advice, and information about the brain disorder that causes muscle tremor, stiffness, and weakness.

67
PHARMACEUTICS

American Pharmaceutical Association
2215 Constitution Avenue, NW
Washington, DC 20037
(800) 237-2742
(202) 628-4410

68
PSYCHIATRY

American Psychiatric Association
1400 K Street, NW
Washington, DC 20005
(202) 682-6000

69
PSYCHOLOGY

American Psychological Association
750 First Street, NE
Washington, DC 20002
(800) 374-2721
(202) 336-5500
(202) 336-6123 tdd

70
RED CROSS;
RELIEF
PROGRAMS

American Red Cross
431 18th Street
Washington, DC 20006
(202) 737-8300

71
REHABILITATION

American Rehabilitation Association
P.O. Box 17675
Washington, DC 20041
(800) 368-3513

72
AIDS; HERPES;
SEXUALLY
TRANSMITTED
DISEASES;
SOCIAL HEALTH;
VENEREAL
DISEASES

American Social Health Association
P.O. Box 13827
Research Triangle Park, NC 27709
(800) 342-2437 NATIONAL AIDS HOTLINE
(800) 243-7889 NATIONAL AIDS HOTLINE
  TTY/TDD
(800) 227-8922 NATIONAL SEXUALLY
  TRANSMITTED DISEASES HOTLINE
(919) 361-8488 HERPES RESOURCE CENTER
  HOTLINE
(919) 361-8400

American Society for Dermatologic
  Surgery
  see American Academy of Dermatology

73
ENDOSCOPY;
GASTRO-
INTESTINAL
DISEASES

American Society of Gastrointestinal
    Endoscopy
13 Elm Street
P.O. Box 1565
Manchester, MA 01944
(508) 526-8330
   While the Society does not provide
information to the general public, it does
provide information to the health care
professional for educating the public.

74
INTERNAL
MEDICINE;
MEDICARE

American Society of Internal Medicine
2011 Pennsylvania Avenue, NW,
    Suite 800
Washington, DC 20006
(800) 338-2746 MEMBERS ONLY, NOT FOR
    THE PUBLIC
(202) 835-2746
   Choices on the automated system
include Medicare regulations, publications, and membership information.

75
PLASTIC
SURGEONS AND
SURGERY;
RECONSTRUCTIVE
SURGEONS AND
SURGERY

American Society of Plastic and
    Reconstructive Surgeons
444 East Algonquin Road
Arlington Heights, IL 60005
(800) 635-0635 PLASTIC SURGERY
    INFORMATION LINE (Recording)
(708) 228-9900

76
CHILDBIRTH;
LAMAZE
(ASPO);
OBSTETRICS;
PSYCHOPRO-
PHYLAXIS IN
OBSTETRICS

American Society for Psychoprophylaxis
    in Obstetrics
1200 19th Street, NW, Suite 300
Washington, DC 20036-2401
(800) 368-4404 ASPO LAMAZE
(202) 857-1128

American Speech-Language-Hearing
Association
see National Association for Hearing
and Speech Action

77
SUDDEN
INFANT DEATH
SYNDROME

American Sudden Infant Death
Syndrome Institute
6065 Roswell Road, Suite 876
Atlanta, GA 30328
(800) 232-7437
(404) 843-1030

American Thoracic Society
see American Lung Association

78
HEARING;
TINNITUS

American Tinnitus Association
P.O. Box 5
Portland, OR 97207
(503) 248-9985
   Provides information about the condition that is characterized by ringing, buzzing, hissing, or other noise in the ear.

79
TRAUMA

American Trauma Society
8903 Presidential Parkway, Suite 512
Upper Marlboro, MD 20772-2656
(800) 556-7890
(301) 420-4189

American Tuberous Sclerosis Association
see Tuberous Sclerosis Association
of America

80
VETERINARY
MEDICINE

American Veterinary Medical
Association
1931 North Meacham Road, Suite 100
Schaumburg, IL 60173
(800) 248-2862
(708) 925-8070

81
AMYOTROPHIC
LATERAL
SCLEROSIS

Amyotrophic Lateral Sclerosis
    Association
21021 Ventura Boulevard, Suite 321
Woodland Hills, CA 91364
(800) 782-4747
(818) 340-7500

Provides assistance and information to those concerned about "Lou Gehrig's disease," a motor neuron disease in which the nerves that control muscular activity degenerate within the brain and spinal cord. This causes weakness and wasting of muscles.

82
ANKYLOSING
SPONDYLITIS

Ankylosing Spondylitis Association
P.O. Box 5872
Sherman Oaks, CA 91413
(800) 777-8189
(818) 981-9826

Provides advice and assistance to those concerned with this inflammatory disease of the joints between vertebrae in the spine and the joints between the spine and the pelvis.

83
ANOREXIA
NERVOSA;
BULEMIA;
EATING
DISORDERS

Anorexia Bulemia Treatment and
    Education Center
6125 Clayton Avenue, Suite 215
St. Louis, MO 63139-3295
(314) 569-6898
(314) 569-6059 TO SPEAK TO A NURSE

84
ANOREXIA
NERVOSA;
BULEMIA; EATING
DISORDERS

Anorexia Nervosa and Associated
    Disorders
Box 7
Highland Park, IL 60035
(708) 831-3438 ANAD HOTLINE

85
RETARDATION

The Arc
500 East Border Street, Suite 300
Arlington, TX 76010
(800) 433-5255
(817) 261-6003
   Formerly known as the Association for
Retarded Citizens.

86
AUTISM

ARRISE, Inc.
9238 Parklane
Franklin Park, IL 60131
(708) 451-2740 VOICE/TDD
   Provides information about autism.

87
ALTERNATIVE
MEDICINE OR
THERAPEUTICS;
ARTHRITIS

Arthritis Consulting Services
4620 North State Road 7, Suite 206
Ft. Lauderdale, FL 33319
(800) 327-3027
(305) 739-3202
   Provides information on holistic
approaches to the treatment of arthritis.

88
ARTHRITIS

Arthritis Foundation
1314 Spring Street, NW
Atlanta, GA 30309
(800) 283-7800 INFORMATION LINE
   (Recording)
(404) 872-7100 (Voice mail)
   Provides information and referral
concerning local chapters.

89
ASBESTOS

Asbestos Ombudsman Clearinghouse
U.S. Environmental Protection Agency
Asbestos Ombudsman, 1230C
401 M Street, SW
Washington, DC 20460
(800) 368-5888 ASBESTOS OMBUDSMAN
   HOTLINE
(703) 305-5938
   Provides information on handling
asbestos and explanation of legislation.

90
ASBESTOS

Asbestos Victim Special Fund Trust
1500 Walnut Street, Suite 1203
Philadelphia, PA 19102
(800) 447-7590
(215) 735-1188
  Provides asbestos information to the public.

91
BLINDNESS;
RETARDATION

Association for the Advancement of the
    Blind and Retarded
164-09 Hillside Avenue
Jamaica, NY 11432-4140
(718) 523-2222

92
PHYSICIANS;
SURGERY

Association of American Physicians and
    Surgeons
1601 North Tucson Boulevard, Suite 9
Tucson, AZ 85716
(800) 635-1196
(602) 327-4885

Association for Brain Tumor Research
  see American Brain Tumor Association

93
CHILDREN

Association for the Care of Children's
    Health
7910 Woodmont Avenue, Suite 300
Bethesda, MD 20814
(301) 654-6549
  Covers psychosocial concerns in children's health.

94
CHILDREN;
RETARDATION

Association for Children with Retarded
    Mental Development
345 Hudson Street
New York, NY 10014
(212) 741-0100
  Unfortunately, to get information from this association, you must write to them.

95
HEALTH

Association of International Health
    Researchers
2665 Pleasant Valley Road
Mobile, AL 36606
(205) 473-3946

96
ENVIRONMENTAL
HEALTH AND
PROTECTION;
OCCUPATIONAL
HEALTH AND
SAFETY

Association of Occupational and
    Environmental Clinics
1010 Vermont Avenue, NW, Suite 513
Washington, DC 20005
(202) 347-4976
    Provides information on occupation-
related problems, such as carpal tunnel
syndrome or light-pen use.

Association for Retarded Citizens
    see The Arc

97
ALLERGY;
ASTHMA

Asthma and Allergy Foundation of
    America
1125 15th Street, NW, Suite 502
Washington, DC 20005
(800) 727-8462 INFORMATION CLEARING-
    HOUSE (Recording)
(202) 466-7643

Back Pain Hotline
    see Texas Back Institute

98
BATTEN'S
DISEASE

Batten's Disease Support and Research
    Association
2600 Parsons Avenue
Columbus, OH 43207
(800) 448-4570
    Provides information and support for
those with this degenerative hereditary
disease.

99
PARENTING;
PREGNANCY

Be Healthy, Inc.
51 Saltrock Road
Baltic, CT 06330
(800) 433-5523 POSITIVE PREGNANCY AND
PARENTING FITNESS MAIL ORDER
CATALOG
(203) 822-8573

100
HEARING

Better Hearing Institute
P.O. Box 1840
Washington, DC 22013
(800) 327-9355 HEARING HELPLINE
(703) 642-0580

101
VISION

Better Vision Institute
1800 North Kent Street, Suite 904
Rosslyn, VA 22209-2152
(800) 424-8422

102
BLINDNESS;
CHILDREN; VISION

Blind Children's Center
4120 Marathon Street
Los Angeles, CA 90029
(800) 222-3566
(213) 664-2153

103
BLINDNESS;
VETERANS, BLIND

Blinded Veterans Association
477 H Street, NW
Washington, DC 20001-2694
(800) 669-7079
(202) 371-8880

104
HAZARDOUS
WASTE; WASTE

Booz-Allen & Hamilton, Inc.
1725 Jefferson Davis Highway
Arlington, VA 22202
(800) 535-0202 EMERGENCY PLANNING/
COMMUNITY RIGHT-TO-KNOW HOTLINES
(800) 553-7672 TDD
(703) 412-9877
   Provides regulatory, policy, and
technical assistance, and information

on availability of documents about
hazardous and solid waste.

105
EPILEPSY

Bowman Gray School of Medicine
Medical Center Boulevard
Winston-Salem, NC 27157-1078
(800) 642-0500 EPILEPSY INFORMATION
   SERVICE
(910) 716-2319

Boys Town
   see Father Flanagan's Boys Town

106
CANCER

Cancer Information Service
Office of Cancer Communications
National Cancer Institute
National Institutes of Health
Building 31, Room 10A24
Bethesda, MD 20892
(800) 422-6237 CANCER INFORMATION
   SERVICE
(301) 496-4000

107
CANCER

Cancer Victors and Friends
National Headquarters
7740 West Manchester, No. 110
Playa Del Rey, CA 90293
(310) 822-5032
   Note: Due to a structural fire,
the temporary address is:
      515 West Sycamore
      El Segundo, CA 90245
   Offers referral to recovered patients
and provides information packets.

108
CANCER;
CHILDREN

Candlelighters Childhood Cancer
      Foundation
7910 Woodmont Avenue, Suite 460
Bethesda, MD 20814
(800) 366-2223
(301) 657-8401

109
CARE; HEALTH
ASSISTANCE;
RELIEF
PROGRAMS

CARE
151 Ellis Street
Atlanta, GA 30303
(800) 422-7385
(404) 681-2552

110
BLINDNESS

Carroll Center for the Blind
770 Centre Street
Newton, MA 02158
(800) 852-3131
(617) 969-6200

111
AIDS; VENEREAL
DISEASES

CAVDA-Citizens AIDS Project
P.O. Box 31915
Chicago, IL 60631-0915
(312) 236-6339
CAVDA is the acronym for Citizen's
Alliance for Venereal Disease Awareness.

112
PERSONALITY
ASSESSMENT;
PSYCHOLOGY

Center for Applications of
        Psychological Type
2815 NW 13th Street, Suite 401
Gainesville, FL 32609
(800) 777-2278
(904) 375-0160

113
OCCUPATIONAL
HEALTH AND
SAFETY

Center for Safety in the Arts
5 Beekman Street, Suite 820
New York, NY 10038
(212) 227-6220
Provides health hazard, safety
training, etc., to all types of artists.

114
AIDS; DISEASE
CONTROL

Centers for Disease Control
1600 Clifton Road, NE
Atlanta, GA 30333
(404) 332-4570 HIV/AIDS STATISTICS
    INFORMATION LINE
Provides statistics, which are updated
quarterly.

115
CHEMICALS

Chemtrek/CMA
Chemical Manufacturer's Association
2501 M Street, NW
Washington, DC 20037
(800) 262-8200 CHEMICAL INFORMATION
HOTLINE–NONEMERGENCY

116
CHILD ABUSE
PREVENTION;
CHILDREN

Child Help USA
6463 Independence Avenue
Woodland Hills, CA 91367
(800) 422-4453 NATIONAL CHILD ABUSE
HOTLINE

117
CHILDREN;
CHILDREN,
MISSING

Childfind of America
P.O. Box 277
New Paltz, NY 12561
(800) 426-5678 MISSING CHILDREN
HOTLINE
(914) 255-1848
Provides support and information
regarding missing children.

118
CHILDREN;
FOSTER HOME
CARE

Childreach
155 Plan Way
Warwick, RI 02886-1099
(800) 556-7918
(401) 738-5600
Assists in finding foster parents for
Third World children.

119
CHILDREN;
CRANIOFACIAL

Children's Craniofacial Association
10210 North Central Expressway
Lockbox 37
Dallas, TX 75231-3404
(800) 535-3643 PATIENT REFERRAL
AND NETWORKING
(214) 368-3590

120
CHILD ABUSE
PREVENTION;
CHILDREN

Children's Defense Fund
25 E Street, NW
Washington, DC 20001
(800) 233-1200
(202) 628-8787

121
CHILDREN;
HOSPICE

Children's Hospice International
700 Princess Street
Alexandria, VA 22314
(800) 242-4453
(703) 684-0330

122
CHILDREN;
DEATH
AND DYING

Children's Wish Foundation
7840 Roswell Road, Suite 301
Atlanta, GA 30350-4867
(800) 323-9474
(404) 393-9474

123
CANCER

City of Hope/Cancer and Major
        Diseases Center
1500 East Duarte Road
Duarte, CA 91010-3000
(800) 423-7119
(818) 359-8111

124
CLEFT PALATE

Cleft Palate Foundation
1218 Grandview Avenue
Pittsburgh, PA 15211
(800) 242-5338
(412) 481-1376

125
COCAINE

Cocaine Anonymous World Services
3740 Overland Avenue, Suite G
Los Angeles, CA 90034
(800) 347-8998
(310) 559-5833
    Provides hotline numbers for each
state.

126
ALTERNATIVE
MEDICINE OR
THERAPEUTICS

Committee for Freedom of Choice in
    Medicine
1180 Walnut Avenue
Chula Vista, CA 91911
(800) 227-4473
(619) 429-8200
    Supports and encourages alternative
health methods.

127
MENTAL HEALTH
AND ILLNESS

Community Mental Health Council, Inc.
8704 South Constance Avenue
Chicago, IL 60617
(312) 734-4033

128
AIDS

Community Provider AIDS Training
San Francisco General Hospital
Building 80, Ward 83
San Francisco, CA 94110
(800) 933-3413 HIV TELEPHONE CONSUL-
    TATION SERVICE (For health care
    providers only)
(415) 476-7070

129
DEATH AND
DYING

The Compassionate Friends
P.O. Box 3696
Oak Brook, IL 60522-3696
(708) 990-0010
    Provides support and information on
death and dying.

130
ADOPTION;
PARENTING

Concerned United Birthparents
2000 Walker Street
Des Moines, IA 50317
(800) 822-2777 (Recording)
(515) 263-9558 (Recording)
    Provides information on support
groups for birth parents who gave up
children.

131
CONSERVATION
OF ENERGY

Conservation and Renewable Energy
    Inquiry and Referral Service
P.O. Box 3048
Merrifield, VA 22116
(800) 523-2929 CONSERVATION AND
    RENEWABLE ENERGY HOTLINE

132
CONSUMER
EDUCATION

Consumer Education Research Center
350 Scotland Road
Orange, NJ 07050
(800) 872-0121
(201) 676-6663

133
CONSUMER
EDUCATION

Consumer Federation of America
1424 16th Street, NW, Suite 604
Washington, DC 20036
(202) 387-6121

134
CONSUMER
EDUCATION;
HEALTH; PATIENT
EDUCATION

Consumer Health Information Research
    Institute
3521 Broadway
Kansas City, MO 64111-2562
(800) 821-6671
(816) 753-8850
    Provides referrals and a patient education library.

Consumer Product Safety Commission
    see United States Consumer Product
    Safety Commission

135
CONTACT LENSES

Contact Lens Manufacturers Association
421 King Street, Suite 224
Alexandria, VA 22314
(800) 343-5367
(800) 344-9060 VIDEO LIBRARY
    INFORMATION (Recording)
(703) 739-0122

136
ANEMIA;
BIRTH DEFECTS;
COOLEY'S
ANEMIA

Cooley's Anemia Foundation
105 East 22nd Street, Suite 911
New York, NY 10010
(800) 221-3571
(212) 598-0911

Provides information and assistance for people who wish to learn more about this inherited blood disorder.

137
AEROBICS

Cooper Institute for Aerobics Research
12330 Preston Road
Dallas, TX 75230
(800) 635-7050
(214) 701-8001

138
BIRTH DEFECTS;
CORNELIA DE
LANGE
SYNDROME

Cornelia de Lange Syndrome
        Foundation
60 Dyer Avenue
Collinsville, CT 06022-1273
(800) 223-8355
(203) 693-0159

Provides information about birth defects caused by Cornelia de Lange syndrome.

Coronary Heart Disease Research
  see American Health Assistance
        Foundation

139
FAMILY HEALTH

Council on Family Health
225 Park Avenue South, 17th Floor
New York, NY 10003
(212) 598-3617

Courage Stroke Network
  see American Heart Association

140
HOMELESS;
SHELTERS

Covenant House
346 West 17th Street
New York, NY 10011-5002
(800) 999-9999 "9-LINE" CRISIS
    COUNSELING HOTLINE
(212) 727-4000
    Provides 24-hour assistance and
temporary shelter for homeless youth.

141
COLITIS;
CROHN'S
DISEASE;
GASTRO-
INTESTINAL
DISEASES

Crohn's and Colitis Foundation of
    America
386 Park Avenue South, 17th Floor
New York, NY 10016-8804
(800) 343-3637
(212) 685-3440
    Provides information and assistance
for people concerned about the inflammatory diseases of the colon (colitis)
and the gastrointestinal tract (Crohn's
disease).

142
CYSTIC FIBROSIS

Cystic Fibrosis Foundation
6931 Arlington Road, Suite 200
Bethesda, MD 20814
(800) 344-4823
(301) 951-4422
    Provides information about cystic
fibrosis, an inherited disease causing a
tendency toward chronic lung infections
and an inability to absorb nutrients
from food.

143
DEAFNESS

Deafness Research Foundation
9 East 38th Street, 7th Floor
New York, NY 10016
(800) 535-3323
(212) 684-6556
(212) 684-6559 TTY/TDD

Delta Society
see Hearing Dog Resource Center of
the Delta Society

144
DEVELOPMENTAL
DISORDERS;
EMOTIONAL
DISORDERS;
MENTAL HEALTH
AND ILLNESS

Devereaux Foundation
19 South Waterloo Road
Devon, PA 19333-0400
(800) 345-1292
(610) 964-3000
  Provides information about the treatment of emotionally, developmentally, and mentally disadvantaged people.

Dial-a-Hearing Screening Test
see Occupational Hearing Service

145
DARE;
DRUG ABUSE

Drug Abuse Resistance Education
  America
P.O. Box 2090
Los Angeles, CA 90051-0090
(800) 223-3273 DARE AMERICA
(310) 215-0575

146
BIRTH DEFECTS;
EASTER SEAL
SOCIETY

Easter Seal Society
2315 Myron Drive
Raleigh, NC 27607-3357
(800) 662-7119
(919) 783-8898

147
CHILDREN;
MATERNITY
HOMES

Edna Gladney Center
2300 Hemphill Street
Fort Worth, TX 76110
(800) 433-2922
(817) 922-6013
  Provides counseling, shelter, and placement information about infants and maternity homes.

148
ENDOMETRIOSIS

Endometriosis Association
8585 North 76th Place
Milwaukee, WI 53223
(800) 992-3636 ENDOMETRIOSIS CRISIS
    COUNSELING
(800) 426-3636 CANADA
(414) 355-2200

149
ALTERNATIVE
MEDICINE OR
THERAPEUTICS;
DENTISTRY;
ENVIRONMENTAL
HEALTH AND
PROTECTION

Environmental Dental Association
9974 Scripps Ranch Boulevard, Suite 36
San Diego, CA 92131
(800) 388-8124
(619) 586-1208
    Provides information about alternatives to mercury dental fillings, including referral to dentists.

Environmental Protection Agency
    see United States Environmental
        Protection Agency

150
EPILEPSY

Epilepsy Foundation of America
4351 Garden City Drive
Landover, MD 20785-2267
(800) 332-1000
(301) 459-3700

Epilepsy Information Service
    see Bowman Gray School of Medicine

Facial Plastic Surgery Information
        Service
    see American Academy of Facial Plastic
        and Reconstructive Surgery

151
COLORECTAL
DISEASES;
POLYPOSIS

Familial Polyposis Registry
Cleveland Clinic Foundation
Department of Colorectal Surgery
9500 Euclid Avenue
Cleveland, OH 44195
(800) 998-4785
(216) 444-6470 FAMILIAL POLYPOSIS
    REGISTRY
(216) 444-2200 CLEVELAND CLINIC
    FOUNDATION

Provides information about polyposis
and maintains a registry of people
with this inherited disorder in which
numerous polyps occur in the colon
and rectum.

152
ABUSE, FAMILIAL;
FAMILY HEALTH;
SUBSTANCE
ABUSE

Families Anonymous
World Service Office
P.O. Box 3475
Culver City, CA 90231-3475
(800) 736-9805
(818) 989-7841

Provides assistance and support in
dealing with any kind of abuse, including substance and personal abuse.

153
ANEMIA;
FANCONI'S
ANEMIA

Fanconi Anemia Research Foundation
1902 Jefferson Street, Suite 1
Eugene, OR 97405
(503) 687-4658

Provides information on Fanconi's
anemia, a rare type of aplastic anemia
where production of all types of blood
cells in the bone marrow is severely
reduced.

154 BOYS TOWN; CHILDREN; FAMILY HEALTH	Father Flanagan's Boys Town 13940 Gutowski Road Boys Town, NE 68010 (800) 448-3000 BOYS TOWN NATIONAL HOTLINE Counselors are available to help children and families.
155 ALTERNATIVE MEDICINE OR THERAPEUTICS; CHILDREN	Feingold Association of the United States P.O. Box 6550 Alexandria, VA 22306 (800) 321-3287 (703) 768-3287 Supports and encourages alternative health methods for treatment of children with learning and behavioral problems.
156 PREGNANCY	First Way Life Center 686 North Broad Street Woodbury, NJ 08096 (800) 848-5683 PREGNANCY HOTLINE (609) 848-1818 Provides confidential pregnancy counseling.
157 HERBALISM	Flower Essence Society P.O. Box 459 Nevada City, CA 95959 (800) 548-0075 (916) 265-9163 Provides information on the health effects of herbs and plants.
158 FOOD AND DRUG ADMINISTRATION	Food and Drug Administration Office of Consumer Affairs 5600 Fishers Lane Rockville, MD 20857 (301) 443-3170 CONSUMER ASSISTANCE

159
FOOD INSPECTION

Food Safety and Inspection Service
Department of Agriculture
Room 2925, South Building
Washington, DC 20250
(800) 535-4555 MEAT AND POULTRY
        FOOD SAFETY HOTLINE
(202) 720-3333

160
FOUNDATIONS

Foundation Center
79 5th Avenue
New York, NY 10003-3076
(800) 424-9836 CUSTOMER SERVICE
(212) 620-4230

Foundation for Fighting Blindness
   see R P Foundation for Fighting
   Blindness

161
HEALTH

Foundation for Health
337 East Avenue
Watertown, NY 13601-3829
(800) 724-7460 NUTRITION AND HEALTH
(315) 782-6664

162
ALZHEIMER'S
DISEASE

French Foundation for Alzheimer's
        Research
11620 Wilshire Boulevard, Suite 820
Los Angeles, CA 90025-1793
(800) 477-2243
(310) 445-4650

Friends Against SIDS
   see American Sudden Infant Death
   Syndrome Institute

163
ECOLOGY;
ENVIRONMENTAL
HEALTH AND PRO-
TECTION; HEALTH

Global Health Action
1712 Clifton Road
P.O. Box 15086
Atlanta, GA 30333
(404) 634-5748

Good Samaritan Project Teen
see Teens Teaching AIDS Prevention

164
HYDROCEPHALUS

Guardians of Hydrocephalus
    Research Foundation
2618 Avenue Z
Brooklyn, NY 11235-2023
(800) 458-8655
(718) 743-4473
    Provides information on hydro-
cephalus, which occurs when excessive
amounts of cerebrospinal fluid accumu-
lates within the skull.

165
DOGS FOR THE
BLIND

Guide Dog Foundation for the Blind
371 East Jericho Turnpike
Smithtown, NY 11787-2976
(800) 548-4337
(516) 265-2121

166
ALTERNATIVE
MEDICINE OR
THERAPEUTICS;
HEALTH

Health Information Network
    International
4527 Montgomery Drive, Suite E
Santa Rosa, CA 95409
(800) 743-6996
(707) 539-3967
    Identifies the latest research and
information on natural health substances, medical conditions, and
treatment alternatives.

167
VOLUNTEERISM,
HEALTH

Health Volunteers Overseas
c/o Washington Station
P.O. Box 65157
Washington, DC 20035-5157
(202) 296-0928
   Provides public health volunteers.

168
HEALTH
INSURANCE;
INSURANCE

Healthcare Financial Management
      Association
2 Westbrook Corporate Center, Suite 700
Westchester, IL 60154
(800) 252-4362 INFORMATION SERVICE
(708) 531-9600

169
CHILDBIRTH;
CHILDREN;
PARENTING

Healthy Mothers, Healthy Babies
      Coalition
409 12th Street SW, Room 309
Washington, DC 20024-2188
(800) 673-8444
(202) 863-2458

170
DEAFNESS;
HEARING

Hear Now
9745 East Hampton Avenue, Room 300
Denver, CO 80231-4923
(800) 648-4327 VOICE/TDD
(303) 758-4919

171
DOGS FOR
THE DEAF

Hearing Dog Resource Center of
      the Delta Society
Century Building, 3rd Floor
321 Burnett Avenue South
Renton, WA 98055-2569
(206) 226-7357

Hearing Helpline
   see Better Hearing Institute

172
CHILDREN;
DISABLED;
HANDICAPPED

Heartspring
2400 Jardine Drive
Wichita, KS 67219-4699
(800) 835-1043
(316) 262-8271
   Previously listed as the Institute of
Logopedics, provides information on
residential programs for multiply handicapped children.

173
INCONTINENCE

Help for Incontinent People
P.O. Box 544
Union, SC 29379
(800) 252-3337
(803) 579-7900

Herpes Resource Center
   see American Social Health Association

174
HANDICAPPED

Higher Education and Adult Training
      for People with Handicaps
Resource Center
1 Dupont Circle, Suite 800
Washington, DC 20036-1193
(800) 544-3284
(202) 939-9320

175
CHILDREN;
HISTIOCYTOSIS

Histiocytosis Association of America
609 New York Road
Glassboro, NJ 08028
(800) 548-2758
(609) 881-4911
   Provides information on a childhood
disease with rapid cell growth in one
bone only, causing swelling and pain.

176 DEATH AND DYING; HOSPICE	Hospice Education Institute 190 Westbrook Road Essex, CT 06426 (800) 331-1620 HOSPICELINK (203) 767-1620
177 GROWTH	Human Growth Foundation 7777 Leesburg Pike, Suite 202 South Falls Church, VA 22043 (800) 451-6434 (703) 883-1773
178 HUNTINGTON'S CHOREA	Huntington's Disease Society of America 140 West 22nd Street, 6th Floor New York, NY 10011-2420 (800) 345-4372 (212) 242-1968 Provides information and referral for people with Huntington's disease.
179 FITNESS AND FITNESS PROFESSIONALS	IDEA: International Association for Fitness Professionals 6190 Cornerstone Court East, Suite 204 San Diego, CA 92121-3773 (800) 999-4332 (619) 535-8979
180 ENVIRONMENTAL HEALTH AND PROTECTION	Indoor Air Quality Information Clearinghouse P.O. Box 37133 Washington, DC 20013-7133 (800) 438-4318 (301) 585-9020
181 DISABLED	Information Center for Individuals with Disabilities 20 Park Plaza, Room 330 Boston, MA 02116 (800) 462-5015

Institute of Logopedics
see Heartspring

182
NUTRITION;
PREVENTIVE
MEDICINE

International Academy of Nutrition
and Preventive Medicine
8 Wildwood Avenue
P.O. Box 18433
Asheville, NC 28814-0433
(704) 258-3243 (Recording)

183
DENTISTRY

International Association for
Dental Research
1111 14th Street, NW, Suite 1000
Washington, DC 20005
(202) 898-1050

184
ANOREXIA
NERVOSA;
BULEMIA;
EATING
DISORDERS

International Association of Eating
Disorders Professionals
123 NW 13th Street, Suite 206
Boca Raton, FL 33432
(800) 800-8126 REFERRAL SERVICE
(407) 338-6494

International Association for Fitness
Professionals
see IDEA

185
CHILDBIRTH

International Association of Parents and
Professionals for Safe Alternatives
in Childbirth
Route 1, Box 646
Marble Hill, MO 63764-9725
(314) 238-2010
    This organization was formerly known
as the National Association of Parents
and Professionals for Safe Alternatives in
Childbirth, and still uses the original
acronym of NAPPSAC.

186
PAIN

International Association for the
Study of Pain
909 NE 43rd Street, Suite 306
Seattle, WA 98105
(206) 547-6409

Educates physicians and health care
practitioners in dealing with patients
in pain.

187
ATHEROSCLERO-
SIS

International Atherosclerosis Society
c/o Barbara Gordin
6550 Fannin, No. 1423
Houston, TX 77030
(713) 790-4226

188
BUNDLE BRANCH
BLOCK;
CARDIOLOGY

International Bundle Branch Block
Association
6631 West 83rd Street
Los Angeles, CA 90045-2899
(310) 670-9132

Provides information on bundle
branch block, a rare heart condition
involving "electrical malfunction,"
for which there is no known cure.

189
ADOPTION;
CHILDREN

International Children's Care
2711 NE 134th Street
Vancouver, WA 98686
(800) 422-7729
(206) 573-0429

Assists with foreign adoptions.

190
MENTAL HEALTH
AND ILLNESS

International Committee Against
Mental Illness
P.O. Box 1921
Grand Central Station
New York, NY 10163
(914) 359-7387

Covers psychosocial rehabilitation
and mental health.

191
EYE AND EYE
DISEASES

International Eye Foundation
7801 Norfolk Avenue, Suite 200
Bethesda, MD 20814
(301) 986-1830

192
ALTERNATIVE
MEDICINE OR
THERAPEUTICS;
BIOENERGETIC
ANALYSIS

International Institute for
    Bioenergetic Analysis
144 East 36th Street
New York, NY 10016
(212) 532-7742
    Studies the health benefits of
biological energy.

193
CONTACT LENSES;
ORTHO-
KERATOLOGY

International Orthokeratology Society
1575 West Big Beaver Road, Suite C-11
Troy, MI 48084
(800) 626-7846
    Provides information on using
contact lenses to correct astigmatism
and myopia.

194
POLIO

International Polio Network
5100 Oakland Avenue, No. 206
St. Louis, MO 63110-1406
(314) 534-0475

195
REHABILITATION

International Rehabilitation
    Medicine Association
1333 Moursund Avenue, Room A-221
Houston, TX 77030
(713) 799-5086

196
RHETT'S
SYNDROME

International Rhett Syndrome
    Association
9121 Piscataway Road, Suite 2-B
Clinton, MD 20735
(301) 856-3334 (Recording)
    Provides support and referral for par-
ents of children suffering from Rhett's
syndrome, which afflicts female babies

(7-18 months) and causes them to become autistic-like.

International Service Association for
Health
see Global Health Action

197
DERMATOLOGY;
SURGERY

International Society for Dermatologic
Surgery
P.O. Box 4014
Schaumburg, IL 60168-4014
(708) 330-0230

198
HEMATOLOGY

International Society of Hematology
920 Hilton
200 1st Street, SW
Rochester, MN 55905
(507) 284-3937

International Society for Prevention of
Child Abuse and Neglect
see Kempe National Center for
Prevention of Child Abuse
and Neglect

199
RESPIRATORY
MEDICINE

International Society for Respiratory
Protection
c/o Brad Squibb
P.O. Box 158
Jonesborough, TN 37659
(615) 753-1388

200
DISABLED;
HANDICAPPED,
EMPLOYMENT

Job Accommodation Network
West Virginia University
918 Chestnut Ridge Road, Suite 1
P.O. Box 6080
Morgantown, WV 26506-6080
(800) 526-7234 NETWORK FOR DISABLED
SEEKING EMPLOYMENT
(304) 293-7186

201
DRUG ABUSE

Just Say No International
2101 Webster Street, Suite 1300
Oakland, CA 94612
(800) 258-2766
(510) 451-6666

202
DIABETES
MELLITUS

Juvenile Diabetes Foundation
    International
432 Park Avenue South, 16th Floor
New York, NY 10016-8013
(800) 223-1138
(800) 533-2873
(212) 889-7575

203
CHILD ABUSE
PREVENTION

Kempe National Center for Prevention
    of Child Abuse and Neglect
1205 Oneida Street
Denver, CO 80220
(303) 321-3963

204
CHILDREN,
MISSING

Kevin Collins Foundation for
    Missing Children
P.O. Box 590473
San Francisco, CA 94159
(800) 272-0012
(415) 771-8477

205
CHILD ABUSE
PREVENTION

Kidsrights
10100 Park Cedar Drive
Charlotte, NC 28210
(800) 892-5437
(704) 541-0100

206
BREAST FEEDING
(LA LECHE)

La Leche League International
1400 North Meacham Road
Schaumburg, IL 60173-4840
(800) 525-3243 ONLY FOR MOTHERS WHO
    NEED HELP
(708) 519-7730 FOR USE BY ALL OTHERS
    Provides information on breast feeding.

207
AMYOTROPHIC
LATERAL
SCLEROSIS

Les Turner Foundation
3325 West Main Street
Skokie, IL 60076
(708) 679-3311 VOICE/TDD
Provides information and support for
people with amyotrophic
lateral sclerosis (ALS).

208
LEUKEMIA

Leukemia Research Foundation
899 Skokie Boulevard, Suite LL14
Northbrook, IL 60062
(312) 275-1177
(708) 480-1177

209
LEUKEMIA

Leukemia Society of America
600 3rd Avenue
New York, NY 10016
(800) 955-4572
(212) 573-8484

210
AGING

Life Extension Foundation
2490 Griffin Road
Fort Lauderdale, FL 33312
(800) 327-6110
(305) 966-4886
Provides information on anti-aging
research.

211
BLINDNESS

The Lighthouse
111 East 59th Street
New York, NY 10022
(800) 334-5497
(212) 808-0077
(212) 808-5544 TTY/TDD
Provides information on vision
and aging.

212 DWARFISM	Little People of America P.O. Box 9897 Washington, DC 20016 (800) 243-9273 DWARF HELPLINE (Recording)
213 ORGAN DONATION	Living Bank P.O. Box 6725 Houston, TX 77265 (800) 528-2971 ORGAN DONOR REGISTRY AND REFERRAL SERVICE (713) 961-9431

	Lung Line
	  see National Jewish Center for
	    Immunology and Respiratory
	    Medicine

214
LUPUS
	Lupus Foundation of America
	4 Research Place, Suite 180
	Rockville, MD 20850-3226
	(800) 558-0121 INFORMATION LINE
	    (Recording)
	(301) 670-9292
	  Provides information on a chronic disease causing inflammation of connective tissue.

215
BIRTH DEFECTS
	March of Dimes Birth Defects
	    Foundation
	National Office
	1275 Mamaroneck Avenue
	White Plains, NY 10605
	(914) 428-7100
	  Note: Most (800) numbers for the March of Dimes are regional or local numbers only. Check your local telephone directory for the (800) number for your area.

216
ORGAN
DONATION

Medic Alert Foundation International
P.O. Box 1009
2323 Colorado Avenue
Turlock, CA 95381-1009
(800) 432-5378 MEDIC ALERT ORGAN
DONOR PROGRAM
(209) 668-3333

217
EAR DISORDERS

Meniere's Network
c/o Ear Foundation at Baptist Hospital
2000 Church Street
Box 111
Nashville, TN 37236
(800) 545-4327 INFORMATION
(Recording)
(615) 329-7809 VOICE/TDD
Provides information on an inner ear
disorder caused by excessive fluid. For
those with touch-tone telephones, the
voice-mail system will direct you to press
2 for Meniere's Network.

218
AIR AMBULANCE

Mercy Medical Airlift
P.O. Box 1940
Manassas, VA 22110
(800) 296-1217 PATIENT AIRLIFT HOTLINE
(703) 361-1191

219
CHILDREN,
MISSING;
RUNAWAYS

Metro-Help
3080 North Lincoln Avenue
Chicago, IL 60657
(800) 621-4000 NATIONAL RUNAWAY
SWITCHBOARD
(800) 344-2785 INFORMATION LINE
(Recording)

220
CHILDREN,
MISSING

Missing Children Help Center
410 Ware Boulevard, Suite 400
Tampa, FL 33619
(800) 872-5437
(813) 623-5437

221
DRUNK DRIVERS

Mothers Against Drunk Drivers
511 East John Carpenter Freeway,
     Suite 700
Irving, TX 75062-8187
(800) 438-6233 VICTIM HOTLINE
(214) 744-6233, extension 247

222
MUSCULAR
DYSTROPHY

Muscular Dystrophy Association
3300 East Sunrise Drive
Tucson, AZ 85718
(800) 572-1717
(602) 529-2000
   Provides information on an inherited
muscle disorder with slow, progressive
degeneration of muscle fiber.

223
MYASTHENIA
GRAVIS

Myasthenia Gravis Foundation
53 West Jackson Boulevard, Suite 660
Chicago, IL 60604
(800) 541-5454
(312) 427-6252
   Provides information on a condition
in which muscles become weak and tire
easily, usually affecting eyes, face, throat,
and limbs.

224
DRUG ABUSE

Narcotics Anonymous
P.O. Box 9999
Van Nuys, CA 91409
(818) 780-3951

225
ABORTION

National Abortion Federation
1436 U Street, NW, Suite 103
Washington, DC 20009
(800) 772-9100 ABORTION HOTLINE
(202) 667-5881

226
ADOPTION

National Adoption Center
1500 Walnut Street, Suite 701
Philadelphia, PA 19102
(800) 862-3678
(215) 735-9988
  Specializes in children with special
needs.

227
ADOPTION

National Adoption Information
    Clearinghouse
11426 Rockville Pike, Suite 410
Rockville, MD 20852
(301) 231-6512

228
AIDS

National AIDS Clearinghouse
P.O. Box 6003
Rockville, MD 20849-6003
(800) 458-5231 INFORMATION
(800) 243-7021 TTY/TDD
(301) 217-0023 INTERNATIONAL CALLS

National AIDS Hotlines
  see American Social Health Association

229
ENVIRONMENTAL
HEALTH AND
PROTECTION

National Air Toxics Information
    Clearinghouse
United States Environmental Protection
    Agency
Office of Air Quality Planning and
    Standards, MD-13
Research Triangle Park, NC 27711
(919) 541-0850
  Collects, classifies, and disseminates
air toxics information.

230
ALLERGY;
ASTHMA

National Allergy and Asthma Network
3554 Chain Bridge Road, Suite 200
Fairfax, VA 22030-2709
(800) 878-4403 ALLERGY AND ASTHMA
    NETWORK
(703) 385-4403

National Alliance of Blind Students
see American Council of the Blind

231
MENTAL HEALTH
AND ILLNESS

National Alliance for the Mentally Ill
2101 Wilson Boulevard, Suite 302
Arlington, VA 22201
(800) 950-6264
(703) 524-7600

232
ALZHEIMER'S
DISEASE; MENTAL
HEALTH AND
ILLNESS

National Alzheimer's Disease and
    Related Disorders Association
919 North Michigan Avenue, Suite 1000
Chicago, IL 60611
(800) 272-3900 EXT. 3699 PUBLICATIONS
    ORDERS
(312) 335-8700
(312) 335-8882 TDD

233
ALCOHOLISM;
COUNSELORS;
DRUG ABUSE

National Association of Alcoholism and
    Drug Abuse Counselors
3717 Columbia Pike, Suite 300
Arlington, VA 22204
(800) 548-0497
(703) 920-4644

234
AGING

National Association of Area Agencies
    on Aging
1112 16th Street, NW, Suite 100
Washington, DC 20036
(800) 677-1116 ELDERCARE LOCATOR
    INFORMATION LINE
(202) 296-8130
    ELDERCARE LOCATOR provides the
name of the nearest area agency for

local services. It is sponsored by the United States Administration on Aging.

235
CRANIOFACIAL;
FACIAL SURGERY

National Association for the Craniofacially Handicapped
P.O. Box 11082
Chattanooga, TN 37401
(800) 332-2373 "FACES" RESOURCE FILES AND INFORMATION
(615) 266-1632

236
CHILDREN

National Association for the Education of Young Children
1509 16th Street, NW
Washington, DC 20036-1426
(800) 424-2460
(202) 232-8777

237
HEARING;
SPEECH

National Association for Hearing and Speech Action
10801 Rockville Pike
Rockville, MD 20852
(800) 638-8255 CONSUMER HELPLINE VOICE/TDD
(301) 897-8682

238
HOSPITALITY
HOUSES

National Association of Hospital Hospitality Houses
4013 West Jackson Street
Muncie, IN 47304
(800) 542-9730
(317) 288-3226

Provides referral and information on hospitality houses of hospitals throughout the United States.

239
MANAGED CARE;
PHYSICIANS

National Association of Managed Care
    Physicians
4435 Waterfront Drive, Suite 101
P.O. Box 4765
Glen Allen, VA 23058-4765
(800) 722-0376
(804) 527-1905

National Association of Parents and
    Professionals for Safe Alternatives
    in Childbirth
  see International Association of
    Parents and Professionals for
    Safe Alternatives in Childbirth

240
BLINDNESS

National Association for Parents of the
    Visually Impaired
P.O. Box 317
Watertown, MA 02272-0317
(800) 562-6265
(617) 972-7441

241
AIDS

National Association of People
    with AIDS
1413 K Street, NW, 8th Floor
Washington, DC 20005
(202) 898-0414
  Provides information and referral to
local chapters.

National Association of Rehabilitation
    Facilities
  see American Rehabilitation
    Association

242
SICKLE CELL DISEASE

National Association for Sickle Cell Disease
3345 Wilshire Boulevard, Suite 1160
Los Angeles, CA 90010-1880
(800) 421-8453
(213) 736-5455

National Asthma Center
see National Jewish Center for Immunology and Respiratory Medicine

243
ATTENTION-DEFICIT DISORDER

National Attention-Deficit Disorder Association
19262 Jamboree Road
Irvine, CA 92715 (For listings of support groups only)
(800) 487-2282 SUPPORT GROUP REFERRAL LINE (Recording)

244
AUTISM

National Autism Hotline
Prichard Building
605 9th Street
P.O. Box 507
Huntington, WV 25710-0507
(304) 525-8014

245
**BLACKS (HEALTH);
MINORITY
HEALTH;
WOMEN, BLACK**

National Black Women's Health Project
1237 Ralph David Abernathy Boulevard, SW
Atlanta, GA 30310
(800) 275-2947 (Recording)
(404) 758-9590 (Recording)

246
**BRAIN DISORDERS
AND INJURIES**

National Brain Injury Research Foundation
1612 K Street, Suite 204
Washington, DC 20006
(202) 331-8445

247
CANCER

National Cancer Institute
9000 Rockville Pike, Suite 414
Bethesda, MD 20892
(800) 422-6237 CANCER INFORMATION
    SERVICE
(301) 496-5583

248
BLACKS IN
THE HEALTH
PROFESSIONS

National Center for the Advancement of
    Blacks in the Health Professions
P.O. Box 21121
Detroit, MI 48221
(313) 345-4480

249
CHILD ABUSE
PREVENTION;
CHILDREN,
MISSING

National Center for Missing and
    Exploited Children
2101 Wilson Boulevard, Suite 550
Arlington, VA 22201
(800) 843-5678
(703) 235-4067

250
STUTTERING

National Center for Stuttering
200 East 33rd Street
New York, NY 10016
(800) 221-2483
(212) 532-1460

251
AGING;
BLINDNESS;
VISION

National Center for Vision and Aging
111 East 59th Street
New York, NY 10022
(800) 334-5497
(212) 808-0077
(212) 808-5544 TTY/TDD

252
DISABLED

National Center for Youth with
    Disabilities
University of Minnesota
Box 721
420 Delaware Street, SE
Minneapolis, MN 55455
(800) 333-6293
(612) 626-2825

National Child Abuse Hotline
see Child Help USA

253
CHILD SAFETY

National Child Safety Council
P.O. Box 1368
Jackson, MI 49204
(800) 222-1464 NATIONAL CHILDWATCH
    CAMPAIGN
(517) 764-6070

254
ALCOHOLISM;
DRUG ABUSE

National Clearinghouse for Alcohol
    and Drug Information
11426 Rockville Pike, Suite 200
Rockville, MD 20852
(800) 729-6686
(800) 487-4889 TDD
(301) 468-2600

255
COCAINE;
DRUG ABUSE

National Cocaine Hotline
P.O. Box 100
Summit, NJ 07902-0100
(800) 262-2463 NATIONAL COCAINE
    HOTLINE

256
CHILD ABUSE
PREVENTION

National Committee to Prevent
    Child Abuse
332 South Michigan Avenue, Suite 1600
Chicago, IL 60604
(800) 835-2671 PUBLICATION ORDERS ONLY
(312) 663-3520

257
AGING

National Council on the Aging
409 3rd Street, SW, 2nd Floor
Washington, DC 20024
(800) 424-9046
(202) 479-1200

258
ALCOHOLISM

National Council on Alcoholism
(800) 622-2255 NATIONAL COUNCIL ON
ALCOHOLISM AND DRUG DEPENDENT
HOPELINE (To identify state affiliate
telephone numbers only; touch
tone telephones only)

see National Clearinghouse for Alcohol
and Drug Information for more
information.

259
CHILD ABUSE PRE-
VENTION; FAMILY
HEALTH

National Council on Child Abuse and
Family Violence
1155 Connecticut Avenue, NW,
Suite 300
Washington, DC 20036
(800) 222-2000 HELPLINE
(202) 429-6695

260
PATIENT
EDUCATION

National Council on Patient
Information and Education
666 Eleventh Street, NW, Suite 810
Washington, DC 20001
(202) 347-6711
Note: This organization prefers that
the public write for information. Do
not call.

261
DOWN
SYNDROME

National Down Syndrome Congress
1605 Chantilly Drive, Suite 250
Atlanta, GA 30324
(800) 232-6372
(404) 633-1555

262
DOWN SYNDROME

National Down Syndrome Society
666 Broadway, 8th Floor
New York, NY 10012
(800) 221-4602
(212) 460-9330

263
EASTER SEAL SOCIETY

National Easter Seal Society
230 West Monroe Street, Suite 1800
Chicago, IL 60606
(800) 221-6827
(312) 726-6200

264
EMERGENCY MEDICINE

National Emergency Medicine
    Association
306 West Joppa Road
Towson, MD 21204
(800) 332-6362
(410) 494-0300

265
EYE AND EYE DISEASES

National Eye Care Project
P.O. Box 429098
San Francisco, CA 94142-9098
(800) 222-3937 MEDICAL AND SURGICAL EYE
    CARE FOR THE ELDERLY

266
EYE AND EYE DISEASES

National Eye Research Foundation
910 Skokie Boulevard, Suite 207A
Northbrook, IL 60062
(800) 621-2258
(708) 564-4652

267
BLINDNESS; HANDICAPPED, EMPLOYMENT

National Federation of the Blind
1800 Johnson Street
Baltimore, MD 21230
(800) 638-7518 JOB OPPORTUNITIES FOR
    THE BLIND
(410) 659-9314

268
FIRE PREVENTION

National Fire Protection Association
1 Batterymarch Park
P.O. Box 9146
Quincy, MA 02269-9101
(800) 344-3555
(617) 770-3000

269
CANCER

National Foundation for Cancer
    Research
7315 Wisconsin Avenue, Suite 500W
Bethesda, MD 20814
(800) 321-2873
(301) 654-1250

270
DEPRESSIVE
ILLNESS

National Foundation for Depressive
    Illness
P.O. Box 2257
New York, NY 10116
(800) 248-4344 INFORMATION AND
    SYMPTOM DESCRIPTIONS (Recording)

271
FACIAL SURGERY;
SURGERY

National Foundation for Facial
    Reconstruction
317 East 34th Street, Suite 901
New York, NY 10016
(800) 422-3223 PATIENT REFERRAL
(212) 263-6656

National Foundation for Ileitis and
    Colitis
    see Crohn's and Colitis Foundation
    of America

272
FRAGILE X;
GENETIC
DISEASES;
MENTAL
RETARDATION

National Fragile X Foundation
1441 York Street, Suite 215
Denver, CO 80206
(800) 688-8765
(303) 333-6155

Provides information on Fragile X,
an inherited genetic defect that causes
mental retardation.

273
GENETIC
DISEASES

National Gaucher Foundation
11140 Rockville Pike, Suite 350
Rockville, MD 20852-3106
(800) 925-8885
(301) 816-1515

Supports research into causes of and
development of treatments and cures for
Gaucher's disease, a genetic condition.

National Glaucoma Research
see American Health Assistance
Foundation

274
ENVIRONMENTAL
HEALTH AND
PROTECTION;
TOXICOLOGY;
WATER

National Ground Water Information
Center
6375 Riverside Drive
P.O. Box 9050
Dublin, OH 43017-0950
(800) 332-2104
(614) 761-3222

275
HEAD INJURY

National Head Injury Foundation
1776 Massachusetts Avenue, NW,
Suite 100
Washington, DC 20036-1904
(800) 444-6443 FAMILY HELPLINE
(202) 296-6443

276
HEADACHE

National Headache Foundation
5252 North Western Avenue
Chicago, IL 60625
(800) 843-2256
(312) 878-7715

277
AIDS;
ALLERGY;
ASTHMA;
CANCER;
DRUG ABUSE;
HEALTH;
MEDICARE

National Health Information Center
Office of Disease Prevention and Health
      Promotion
United States Department of Health
      and Human Services
P.O. Box 1133
Washington, DC 20013-1133
(800) 336-4797
(301) 565-4167

Helps locate sources of information
on health matters, both traditional and
alternative practices, including AIDS,
cancer, Medicare, drug abuse, asthma,
and allergies.

278
HEARING

National Hearing Aid Society
20361 Middlebelt Road
Livonia, MI 48152
(800) 521-5247 HEARING AID HELPLINE
(313) 478-2610

279
HEMOPHILIA

National Hemophilia Foundation
110 Greene Street, Suite 303
New York, NY 10012
(800) 424-2634 HANDI INFORMATION LINE
(212) 219-8180

280
ACCIDENT
PREVENTION;
AUTOMOBILE
SAFETY

National Highway Traffic Safety
      Administration
400 7th Street, SW, Room 5319
Washington, DC 20590
(800) 424-9393 AUTO SAFETY HOTLINE

281
HOSPICE

National Hospice Organization
1901 North Moore Street, Suite 901
Arlington, VA 22209
(800) 658-8898
(703) 243-5900

282
CHILDREN;
DISABLED

National Information Center for
Children and Youth with Disabilities
P.O. Box 1492
Washington, DC 20013-1492
(800) 999-5599 INFORMATION AND ORDERS
(Recording)
(703) 893-6061
(703) 893-6814 TTY/TDD

283
CHILDREN;
DISABLED

National Information Clearinghouse
for Infants with Disabilities and
Life-Threatening Conditions
Center for Developmental Disabilities
University of South Carolina
Benson Building
Columbia, SC 29208
(800) 922-9234, EXT. 201 VOICE/TDD
(803) 777-6222
(803) 777-4435

284
VETERANS,
VIETNAM

National Information System for
Vietnam Veterans and Their
Families
Center for Developmental Disabilities
University of South Carolina
Benson Building
Columbia, SC 29208
(800) 922-9234, EXT. 201 VOICE/TDD
(803) 777-6222
(803) 777-4435

285
AIDS

National Institutes of Health
Intramural AIDS Program
Building 10, Room 7D43
Bethesda, MD 20892
(800) 243-7644 AIDS CLINICAL TRIALS
INFORMATION
Provides National Institutes of Health
AIDS ongoing clinical trial information
for health professionals and the public.

286 HOSPICE	National Institute for Jewish Hospice 8723 Alden Drive, Suite 652 Los Angeles, CA 90048 (800) 446-4448 INFORMATION 　　(Recording) (310) 854-3036
287 OCCUPATIONAL HEALTH AND SAFETY	National Institute for Occupational 　　Safety and Health 4676 Columbia Parkway Cincinnati, OH 45226-1998 (800) 356-4674
288 IMMUNOLOGY; RESPIRATORY MEDICINE	National Jewish Center for Immunology 　　and Respiratory Medicine 1400 Jackson Street Denver, CO 80206 (800) 222-5864 LUNG LINE INFORMATION 　　SERVICE (Recording) (303) 388-4461
289 KIDNEY AND KIDNEY DISEASE	National Kidney Foundation 30 East 33rd Street, Suite 1100 New York, NY 10016 (800) 622-9010 (212) 889-2210
290 ENVIRONMENTAL HEALTH AND PROTECTION; LEAD	National Lead Information Center (Address not available) (800) 532-3394 (Recording) (800) 526-5456 TDD 　　Leave name and number to receive a packet of information.
291 NURSES AND NURSING	National League for Nursing 350 Hudson Street New York, NY 10014 (800) 669-1656 (212) 989-9393

292
LEUKEMIA

National Leukemia Association
585 Stewart Avenue, Suite 536
Garden City, NY 11530
(516) 222-1944

293
LYMPHEDEMA

National Lymphedema Network
Aurora Medical Clinic
2211 Post Street, Suite 404
San Francisco, CA 94115
(800) 541-3259 INFORMATION
(Recording)
(415) 921-2911
    Provides information on lymph-
edema, an abnormal accumulation of
lymph fluids in tissues, causing swelling
of a limb.

294
MARFAN
SYNDROME

National Marfan Foundation
382 Main Street
Port Washington, NY 11050
(800) 862-7326
(516) 883-8712
    Provides information on Marfan syn-
drome, an inherited disorder of connec-
tive tissue resulting in abnormalities of
the skeleton, heart, and eyes.

295
BONE MARROW
DONORS;
MARROW
DONORS;
ORGAN
DONATION

National Marrow Donor Program
3433 Broadway Street, NE, Suite 400
Minneapolis, MN 55413-1762
(800) 627-7692
(612) 378-2044
    Maintains a registry of bone marrow
donors.

296
HEALTH
INSURANCE

National Medi-Card Systems
1070 Commerce Street, Suite F
San Marco, CA 92069
(800) 266-1787
(619) 744-1787

297
MENTAL HEALTH AND ILLNESS

National Mental Health Association
1021 Prince Street
Alexandria, VA 22314-2971
(800) 969-6642 ORDERS FOR PUBLICATIONS
    (Recording)
(800) 433-5959 ORDERS FOR PUBLICATIONS
(703) 684-7722

298
AIDS; BLACKS (HEALTH); MINORITY HEALTH

National Minority AIDS Council
300 I Street, NE, Suite 400
Washington, DC 20002
(202) 544-1076

299
MULTIPLE SCLEROSIS

National Multiple Sclerosis Society
733 3rd Avenue, 6th Floor
New York, NY 10017-3288
(800) 532-7667 INFORMATION
(212) 986-3240

300
AIDS; NATIVE AMERICANS

National Native American AIDS
    Prevention Center
3515 Grand Avenue, Suite 100
Oakland, CA 94610
(800) 283-2437 INDIAN AIDS NETWORK
(510) 444-2051

301
NEUROFIBRO-MATOSIS

National Neurofibromatosis Foundation
141 5th Avenue, Suite 7-S
New York, NY 10010-7105
(800) 323-7938
(212) 460-8980

Provides information on neurofibromatosis, also known as "von Recklinghausen's disease," an inherited disorder
with many soft, fibrous swellings that
grow mostly from nerves in the skin.

302
ALBINISM;
HYPO-
PIGMENTATION

National Organization for Albinism
   and Hypopigmentation
1500 Locust Street, Suite 29
Philadelphia, PA 19102-4415
(800) 473-2310 INFORMATION
   (Recording)
(215) 545-2322

303
DISABLED

National Organization on Disability
910 16th Street, NW, Suite 600
Washington, DC 20006
(800) 248-2253
(202) 293-5960

304
RARE DISEASES

National Organization for Rare
   Disorders
P.O. Box 8923
New Fairfield, CT 06812-1783
(800) 999-6673
(203) 746-6518

National Osteopathic Foundation
   see American Osteopathic Association

305
OSTEOPOROSIS

National Osteoporosis Foundation
1150 17th Street, NW, Suite 500
Washington, DC 20036
(800) 223-9994
(202) 223-2226

306
PARKINSON'S
DISEASE

National Parkinson Foundation
1501 NW 9th Avenue
Miami, FL 33136
(800) 327-4545
(305) 547-6666
   Provides doctor and support group
referrals.

307
ENVIRONMENTAL
HEALTH AND
PROTECTION;
PESTICIDES

National Pesticide Telecommunications
    Network
(Address not available)
(800) 858-7378 FOR THE GENERAL PUBLIC
(800) 858-7377 FOR MEDICAL AND
        GOVERNMENT PERSONNEL
    Provides information concerning
pesticides.

308
RADON

National Radon Hotline
P.O. Box 33435
Washington, DC 20035-0435
(800) 767-72366 OR (800) SOS-RADON
        NATIONAL RADON HOTLINE
    Leave name and address for a
brochure about radon.

309
BIOETHICS;
ETHICS, MEDICAL

National Reference Center for
    Bioethics Literature
Joseph and Rose Kennedy Institute
    of Ethics
Georgetown University
Washington, DC 20057-1065
(800) 633-3849 BIOETHICS REFERENCE
        CENTER
(202) 687-3885

310
REHABILITATION

National Rehabilitation Information
    Center
8455 Colesville Road, Suite 935
Silver Spring, MD 20910-3319
(800) 346-2742
(301) 588-9284

311
CHILD ABUSE
PREVENTION

National Resource Center on Child
    Sexual Abuse
107 Lincoln Street
Huntsville, AL 35801
(800) 543-7006
(205) 534-6868

312
HOMELESS;
MENTAL HEALTH
AND ILLNESS

National Resource Center on
      Homelessness and Mental Illness
262 Delaware Avenue
Delmar, NY 12054
(800) 444-7415
(516) 439-7415

313
ENVIRONMENTAL
HEALTH AND
PROTECTION;
HAZARDOUS
WASTE

National Response Center
United States Coast Guard Headquarters
2100 Second Street, SW, Room 2611
Washington, DC 20593-0001
(800) 424-8802
(202) 267-2675
    Provides a 24-hour facility to report oil
spills, hazardous waste releases, and
other environmental emergencies.

National Retinitis Pigmentosa
      Foundation
   see R P Foundation for Fighting
    Blindness

314
REYE'S
SYNDROME

National Reye's Syndrome
      Foundation, Inc.
P.O. Box 829
Bryan, OH 43506
(800) 233-7393 INFORMATION HOTLINE
(419) 636-2679
    Provides information on Reye's
syndrome, which involves brain and liver
damage after chicken pox, flu, or upper
respiratory tract infection.

National Runaway Switchboard
   see Metro-Help

315
ACCIDENT
PREVENTION;
SAFETY

National Safety Council
1121 Spring Lake Drive
Itasca, IL 60143-3201
(800) 621-7619
(708) 285-1121

316
SARCOIDOSIS

National Sarcoidosis Family Aid and
    Research Foundation
P.O. Box 22868
760 Clinton Avenue
Newark, NJ 07108
(800) 223-6429 INFORMATION
    (Recording)
    Provides information on a rare disease
involving inflammation in lymph nodes
and other body tissues, usually in
young adults.

317
AIDS

National Sheriffs' Association
1450 Duke Street
Alexandria, VA 22314-3490
(800) 424-7827 AIDS PROJECT INFORMATION
(703) 836-7827

318
SJOGREN'S
SYNDROME

National Sjogren's Syndrome
    Association
3201 West Evans Drive
Phoenix, AZ 85023
(800) 395-6772
(602) 516-0787
    Provides information on a syndrome
that causes excessive dryness in the eyes,
mouth, and vagina of mostly middle-
aged, often post-menopausal women.

319
CONSUMER
EDUCATION;
HEALTH
ASSISTANCE

National Society of Patient
    Representation and Consumer
    Affairs
The American Hospital Association
840 North Lake Shore Drive
Chicago, IL 60611
(312) 280-6000

320
BLINDNESS

National Society to Prevent Blindness
500 East Remington Road
Schaumburg, IL 60173
(800) 221-3004
(800) 331-2020
(708) 843-2020

321
SPASMODIC
TORTICOLLIS

National Spasmodic Torticollis
    Association
P.O. Box 476
Elm Grove, IL 53122-0476
(800) 487-8385
    Provides information for people
afflicted with an involuntary twitching
of muscles.

322
SPINAL CORD
INJURIES

National Spinal Cord Injury Association
600 West Cummings Park, Suite 2000
Woburn, MA 01801
(800) 962-9629 MEMBER HOTLINE ONLY
(617) 935-2722

National STD Hotline
    see American Social Health Association

323
STROKE

National Stroke Association
8480 East Orchard Road, Suite 1000
Englewood, CO 80111-5015
(800) 787-6537
(303) 771-1700

National Sudden Infant Death
Syndrome Foundation
see SIDS Alliance

324
TUBEROUS
SCLEROSIS

National Tuberous Sclerosis Association
8000 Corporate Drive, Suite 120
Landover, MD 20785
(800) 225-6872
(301) 459-9888

Provides information on an inherited disorder of the skin and nervous system that usually exhibits acne-like conditions on the face, often with epilepsy, mental retardation, and sometimes non-cancerous tumors.

325
ALTERNATIVE
MEDICINE OR
THERAPEUTICS;
WELLNESS

National Wellness Institute
1045 Clark Street, Suite 210
Stevens Point, WI 54481
(800) 243-8694
(715) 342-2969

326
HEARING

Occupational Hearing Service
P.O. Box 1880
Media, PA 19063
(800) 222-3277 DIAL-A-HEARING
SCREENING TEST

Provides local telephone numbers for screening tests.

327
ENVIRONMENTAL
HEALTH AND
PROTECTION

Office of Environmental Equity
United States Environmental Protection
Agency
401 M Street, SW, 3610
Washington, DC 20460
(800) 962-6215
(202) 260-6357

Works with other EPA offices to address the environmental impacts on "people of color" and low-income populations. Coordinates communication, outreach, education, and training, etc.

328
BLACKS (HEALTH);
MINORITY
HEALTH

Office of Minority Health Resource
    Center
P.O. Box 37337
Washington, DC 20013-7337
(800) 444-6472

329
ENVIRONMENTAL
HEALTH AND
PROTECTION;
WASTE

Office of Underground Storage Tanks
United States Environmental
    Protection Agency
OS-305
401 M Street, SW
Washington, DC 20460
(800) 424-9346 OUST HOTLINE
(800) 553-7672 TDD
    Automated system routes callers to
information about EPA regulations,
current developments and changes,
requests for relevant documents, and
referrals to other agencies.

330
PODIATRY

Ohio College of Podiatric Medicine
10515 Carnegie Avenue
Cleveland, OH 44106
(800) 238-7903
(216) 231-3300

331
DYSLEXIA

Orton Dyslexia Society
P.O. Box 9888
Baltimore, MD 21284
(800) 222-3123 INFORMATION
    (Recording)
(410) 296-0232
    Provides information on support
networks and resources.

332
EATING
DISORDERS

Overeaters Anonymous
World Services Office
P.O. Box 44020
Rio Rancho, NM 87174-4020
(505) 891-2664
 Suggests you check the white pages of your local telephone book for local chapters.

333
OPHTHALMOLOGY

Pan-American Association of
 Ophthalmology
1301 South Bowen Road, Suite 365
Arlington, TX 76013-2286
(817) 265-2831

334
HEALTH

Pan American Health Organization
525 23rd Street, NW
Washington, DC 20037
(202) 861-3200

335
PARENTING

Parents Anonymous
520 South Lafayette Park Place,
 Suite 316
Los Angeles, CA 90057
(800) 421-0353 INFORMATION
 (Recording)
(800) 775-1134 TO START A GROUP
(213) 388-6685

336
DRUG ABUSE

Parents' Resource Institute for Drug
 Education
10 Park Place, Suite 340
Atlanta, GA 30303
(404) 577-4500

337
CHIROPRACTICS

Parker Chiropractic Resource Foundation
P.O. Box 40444
Fort Worth, TX 76140-0444
(800) 950-8044
(817) 293-6444

338
PARKINSON'S DISEASE

Parkinson's Educational Program USA
3900 Birch Street, Suite 105
Newport Beach, CA 92660
(800) 344-7872 INFORMATION
        (Recording)
(714) 250-2975

339
CHILDREN; DISABLED

Pathways Awareness Foundation
123 North Wacker Drive
Chicago, IL 60606
(800) 955-2445 (Recording)
    Provides information on detection of disabilities in early childhood.

340
AIDS; CHILDREN

Pediatric AIDS Foundation
1311 Colorado Avenue
Santa Monica, CA 90404
(310) 395-9051

341
HEALTH; PROJECT HOPE

People to People Health Foundation
Project HOPE Health Sciences
        Education Center
Millwood, VA 22646
(800) 544-4673
(703) 837-2100
    Provides health-related humanitarian assistance and promotes better world health through training of health personnel in developing areas of the world, including the Americas, Africa, Asia, and Eastern Europe.

342
ALTERNATIVE MEDICINE OR THERAPEUTICS; HEALTH

People's Medical Society
462 Walnut Street
Allentown, PA 18102
(800) 624-8773
(215) 770-1670
    Supports and promotes alternative health methods.

343
PESTICIDES

Pesticide Action Network
116 New Montgomery Street, Suite 810
San Francisco, CA 94105
(415) 541-9140

344
PHARMACY

Pharmacy Management Services, Inc.
P.O. Box 30054
Tampa, FL 33630-3054
(800) 237-7676 PHARMACY ASSISTANCE
   SERVICES
(813) 626-7788

345
BURNS

Phoenix Society for Burn Survivors
11 Rust Hill Road
Levittown, PA 19056-2311
(800) 888-2876
(215) 946-2876
   Provides information on self-help
services for burn survivors.

346
CANCER;
MEDICINE;
NUTRITION;
PHYSICIANS;
PREVENTIVE
MEDICINE

Physicians Committee for Responsible
   Medicine
P.O. Box 6322
Washington, DC 20015
(800) 875-4837 U.S. LIVES INFORMATION
   LINE (Recording)
   Provides free listings of sources of
information on nutrition, preventive
medicine, and cancer survival.

347
INSURANCE;
PHYSICIANS

Physicians Who Care Insurance Institute
215 East Quincy, Suite 305
San Antonio, TX 78215
(800) 545-9305
(210) 226-1400
   Provides information on, and patient
education programs for, choosing
appropriate health care plans (such as
health maintenance organizations) or
physician-patient relationships.

348
TRANS-
PLANTATION

Pittsburgh Transplant Foundation
204 Sigma Drive, RIDC Park
Pittsburgh, PA 15230
(800) 366-6777
(412) 963-3550

349
CHILDBIRTH;
PARENTING

Planned Parenthood Federation
    of America
810 7th Avenue
New York, NY 10019
(800) 829-7732
(212) 541-7800

350
PHARMACEUTICS;
PHARMACY

PMS Access
Madison Pharmacy Associates
P.O. Box 9326
Madison, WI 53715
(800) 222-4767 INFORMATION
    (Recording)
(800) 558-7046 TO TALK TO A
    PHARMACIST
(608) 257-8682

351
POLIO

Polio Society
P.O. Box 106273
Washington, DC 20016
(301) 897-8180
    Provides information for polio
survivors and health professionals.

352
GAYS; LESBIANS

Pride Institute
14400 Martin Drive
Eden Prairie, MN 55344
(800) 547-7433
(612) 934-7554
    Provides gay and lesbian medical
services, counseling, and addiction
treatment.

353
AIDS; DRUGS,
EXPERIMENTAL

Project Inform
1965 Market Street, Suite 220
San Francisco, CA 94103
(800) 822-7422 EXPERIMENTAL DRUGS
    HOTLINE
(415) 558-8669

Identifies treatment options, experimental drugs, advocacy and outreach, and organizations for AIDS, ARC, and HIV.

354
BLINDNESS

Recording for the Blind
20 Roszel Road
Princeton, NJ 08540
(800) 221-4792 (Book inquiries only)
(609) 452-0606

355
MENTAL HEALTH
AND ILLNESS

Recovery Incorporated: The Association
    of Nervous and Former Mental
    Patients
802 North Dearborn Street
Chicago, IL 60610
(312) 337-5661

Provides information on controlling temperamental behavior and on changing attitudes toward nervous symptoms and fears.

356
IMPOTENCE

Recovery of Male Potency
27211 Lasher Road, Suite 208
Southfield, MI 48034
(800) 835-7667 TEL-ROMP
(313) 357-1314

Gray's Hospital Impotence Treatment Center provides information and referrals on impotence.

357
REHABILITATION

Rehabilitation International
25 East 21st Street, 4th Floor
New York, NY 10010
(212) 420-1500

358
RESEARCH,
MEDICAL

Research!America
1522 King Street
Alexandria, VA 22314
(800) 366-2873
(703) 739-2577
  Advocates for medical research
through public education.

359
BLINDNESS

Research to Prevent Blindness
598 Madison Avenue, 10th Floor
New York, NY 10022-1614
(800) 621-0026
(212) 752-4333

360
ENVIRONMENTAL
HEALTH AND
PROTECTION

Resource Conservation and
    Recovery Act
United States Environmental
    Protection Agency
OS-305
401 M Street, SW
Washington, DC 20460
(800) 424-9346 RCRA HOTLINE
(800) 553-7672 TDD
  Automated system routes callers to
information about EPA regulations,
current developments and changes,
requests for relevant documents, and
referrals to other agencies.

361
BLINDNESS;
RETINITIS
PIGMENTOSA

R P Foundation for Fighting Blindness
1401 Mount Royal Avenue, 4th Floor
Baltimore, MD 21217-4245
(800) 683-5555
(410) 225-9400

362
ENVIRONMENTAL
HEALTH AND
PROTECTION;
WATER

Safe Drinking Water Hotline
Office of Ground Water and
    Drinking Water
4601
Resource Center
401 M Street, SW
Washington, DC 20460
(800) 426-4791 SAFE DRINKING WATER
    HOTLINE

Saint Jude Children's Research Hospital
    see St. Jude Children's Research
        Hospital

363
SCLERODERMA

Scleroderma Federation
1182 Teaneck Road, Suite 104
Teaneck, NJ 07666-4825
(201) 837-9826
    Provides information on a rare auto-
immune disorder in which the body's
immune system attacks its own tissues.

364
SCLERODERMA

Scleroderma Research Foundation
P.O. Box 200
Columbus, NJ 08022-0200
(800) 637-4005
(609) 261-2200

365
BURNS;
CHILDREN;
DISABLED;
ORTHOPEDICS

Shriners Hospital for Crippled Children
2900 Rocky Point Drive
Tampa, FL 33607-1435
(800) 237-5055 REFERRAL LINE FOR
    ORTHOPEDIC OR BURN CARE
(800) 361-7256 CANADA
(813) 281-0300

366
SUDDEN INFANT
DEATH
SYNDROME

SIDS Alliance
10500 Little Patuxent Parkway, Suite 420
Columbia, MD 21044
(800) 221-7437
(410) 964-8000

Provides support and assistance for persons dealing with Sudden Infant Death Syndrome.

367
INCONTINENCE

Simon Foundation
P.O. Box 815
Wilmette, IL 60091
(800) 237-4666
(708) 864-3913

Provides information and referrals on incontinence.

368
SMOKING
CESSATION

Smokenders
4455 East Camelback Road, Suite D155
Phoenix, AZ 85018
(800) 828-4357
(602) 840-7414

369
SOCIAL
SECURITY

Social Security Administration
Office of Public Inquiries
6401 Security Boulevard
Baltimore, MD 21235
(800) 772-1213
(410) 965-7700

370
ECOLOGY

Society for Human Ecology
c/o Jonathan G. Taylor
National Biological Survey
Midcontinental Ecological Science
    Center
4512 McMurray Avenue
Ft. Collins, CO 80525-3400
(303) 226-9438

Studies the impact of humans on the environment.

Society of Teachers of Family Medicine
see American Academy of Family
Physicians

371
SPINA BIFIDA

Spina Bifida Association of America
4590 MacArthur Boulevard, NW,
Suite 250
Washington, DC 20007-4226
(800) 621-3141
(202) 944-3285

Spinal Cord Injury Hotlines
see American Paralysis Association

372
SPINAL CORD
INJURIES

Spinal Cord Society
Wendell Road
Fergus Falls, MN 56537
(218) 739-5252

Star Center
see Recovery of Male Potency

373
CHILDREN

St. Jude Children's Research Hospital
501 St. Jude Place
Memphis, TN 38105-1942
(800) 238-6030
(800) 645-7900
(800) 877-5833
(901) 522-9733

374
STURGE-WEBER
SYNDROME

Sturge-Weber Foundation
P.O. Box 460931
Aurora, CO 80046
(800) 627-5482
(303) 360-7290
  Provides information on this rare
congenital disorder affecting the skin
and brain, and involving malformation
of blood vessels.

Sudden Infant Death Syndrome Alliance
see SIDS Alliance

375
ENVIRONMENTAL
HEALTH AND
PROTECTION;
WASTE

Superfund Hotline
United States Environmental Protection
    Agency
OS-305
401 M Street, SW
Washington, DC 20460
(800) 424-9346 SUPERFUND HOTLINE
(800) 553-7672 TDD
    Automated system routes callers to
information about EPA regulations,
current developments and changes,
requests for relevant documents, and
referrals to other agencies.

376
BREAST CANCER;
CANCER

Susan G. Komen Breast Cancer
    Foundation
111 Park Forest Shopping Center
Dallas, TX 75234
(800) 462-9273 INFORMATION
    (Recording)

377
DIETETICS;
WEIGHT
CONTROL

Take Off Pounds Sensibly
4575 South 5th Street
Milwaukee, WI 53207
(800) 932-8677
(414) 482-4620
    A noncommercial weight-control
organization that provides support
groups in various areas.

378
AIDS

Teens Teaching AIDS Prevention
3030 Walnut Street
Kansas City, MO 64108
(800) 234-8336
(816) 561-8784
    Counseling from a teen perspective.

379
BACKACHE

Texas Back Institute
3801 West 15th Street
Plano, TX 75075
(800) 247-2225 BACK PAIN HOTLINE
(214) 867-2225

380
ENVIRONMENTAL
HEALTH AND
PROTECTION

Together Foundation for Global Unity
Organization Headquarters
130 South Willar Street
Burlington, VT 05401
(800) 326-5463 ECOLINE
(802) 862-2030

An environmental hotline, ECOLINE
also provides referrals to organizations
and results of environmental and
humanitarian projects.

381
PARENTING

Toughlove, International
P.O. Box 1069
Doylestown, PA 18901
(800) 333-1069 PARENT REFERRAL
SERVICE
(215) 384-7090

382
TOURETTE
SYNDROME

Tourette Syndrome Association
42-40 Bell Boulevard
Bayside, NY 11361-2874
(800) 237-0717
(718) 224-2999

Provides information on a disorder
characterized by repetitive grimaces, tics,
and involuntary noises.

383
CHILDREN;
DEAFNESS;
HEARING

Tripod Grapevine
2901 North Keystone Street
Burbank, CA 91504
(800) 352-8888
(818) 972-2080

Provides information for parents
raising hearing-impaired children.

384
CEREBRAL PALSY

United Cerebral Palsy Associations, Inc.
1522 K Street, NW, Suite 1112
Washington, DC 20005-1202
(800) 872-5827
(202) 842-1266

385
LEUKO-
DYSTROPHY

United Leukodystrophy Foundation
2304 Highland Drive
Sycamore, IL 60178
(800) 728-5483
(815) 895-3211
　　Provides information on an inherited childhood disease in which the sheaths around nerves are destroyed.

386
CHILDREN;
RELIEF
PROGRAMS;
UNICEF

United Nations Children's Fund
　　(Fonds des Nations Unies pour l'Enfance)
3 United Nations Plaza
New York, NY 10017
(212) 326-7000
　　Known as UNICEF, from the former name, United Nations International Children's Emergency Fund.

387
ORGAN
DONATION

United Network for Organ Sharing
P.O. Box 13770
1100 Boulders Parkway, Suite 500
Richmond, VA 23225-8770
(800) 243-6667 ORGAN DONOR HOTLINE
(804) 330-8500

388
SCLERODERMA

United Scleroderma Foundation
P.O. Box 399
Watsonville, CA 95077-0399
(800) 722-4673
(408) 728-2202

389
SAFETY

United States Consumer Product Safety
    Commission
5401 Westbard Avenue
Bethesda, MD 20207
(800) 638-2772 CONSUMER PRODUCT
    SAFETY HOTLINE
(800) 638-8270 TDD

390
MEDICARE;
RADON

United States Department of Health and
    Human Services
Healthcare Financing Administration
6325 Security Boulevard
Baltimore, MD 21207
(800) 638-6833 MEDICARE HOTLINE
    (Recording)

391
HAZARDOUS
WASTE; WASTE

United States Environmental Protection
    Agency
401 M Street, SW
Washington, DC 20460
(800) 535-0202 EMERGENCY PLANNING/
    COMMUNITY RIGHT-TO-KNOW HOTLINES
(703) 412-9877 HOTLINE TOLL NUMBER
(202) 260-2090

392
PHARMACEUTICS

United States Pharmacopeial
    Convention
12601 Twinbrook Parkway
Rockville, MD 20852
(800) 227-8772 CUSTOMER SERVICE
    DEPARTMENT (Recording)
(301) 881-0666

393
AIDS

United States Public Health Service
AIDS Treatment Information Service
P.O. Box 6303
Rockville, MD 20849-6303
(800) 448-0440 HIV-AIDS TREATMENT
    INFORMATION SERVICE

This hotline is supported by the
Centers for Disease Control, the
National Library of Medicine, and a
number of other subsidiaries of the
United States Public Health Service. It
became operative on October 31, 1994.

Us Too
   see American Foundation for
      Urologic Disease

Usher Syndrome Self-Help Network
   see R P Foundation for Fighting
      Blindness

394
CHILDREN,
MISSING

Vanished Children's Alliance
1407 Parkmoor Avenue, Suite 200
San Jose, CA 95126
(800) 826-4743
(408) 971-4822

395
ABUSE, FAMILIAL;
FAMILY HEALTH

Victim's Services
2 Lafayette Street
New York, NY 10007
(212) 577-5500
   Provides information about and
support for victims of domestic violence.

396
VISION

Vision Council of America
1800 North Kent Street, Suite 904
Rosslyn, VA 22209-2152
(800) 424-8422
(703) 243-1508

397
NURSES,
VISITING;
VISITING NURSES

Visiting Nurse Association of America
3801 East Florida Avenue, Suite 900
Denver, CO 80210
(800) 426-2547
(303) 753-0218

398
WELLNESS

Wellness Associates
21489 Orr Springs Road
Ukiah, CA 95482
(707) 937-2331

399
SPORTS
MEDICINE;
WOMEN

Women's Sports Foundation
Eisenhower Park
East Meadow, NY 11554
(800) 227-3988 INFORMATION AND
    REFERRAL SERVICE
(516) 542-4700

400
HEALTH;
MENTAL HEALTH
AND ILLNESS

World Federation for Mental Health
1021 Prince Street
Alexandria, VA 22314
(703) 838-7543

401
HEALTH

World Health Organization
Regional Office for The Americas/
   Pan American Sanitary Bureau
   (AMRO)
525 23rd Street, NW
Washington, DC 20037
(202) 861-3200

402
BLINDNESS

Xavier Society for the Blind
154 East 23rd Street
New York, NY 10010
(800) 637-9193
(212) 473-7800

403
BREAST CANCER

Y-Me National Organization for Breast
   Cancer Information and Support
212 West Van Buren
Chicago, IL 60607
(800) 221-2141 Y-ME HOTLINE
(312) 986-8228

404
CHILD ABUSE
PREVENTION;
CHILDREN

Youth Development International
P.O. Box 178408
San Diego, CA 92177-8408
(800) 448-4663 NATIONAL YOUTH CRISIS
     HOTLINE
(619) 292-5683
    Also known as the "Hit Home"
hotline for the telephone number
(800) HIT-HOME.

Beatrice Kovacs is associate professor in the Department of Library and Information Studies at the University of North Carolina at Greensboro. She is the former collection development librarian at the Medical Center Library, University of New Mexico and at the Medical College of Georgia Library and is the author of *The Decision-Making Process for Library Collections* and co-author of *Using Science and Technology Information Sources.*